Richard W.E. Perrin

Historic Wisconsin Buildings:
A Survey in Pioneer Architecture 1835-1870

Second Edition, Revised

Milwaukee Public Museum

*Other books by the author
published by the Milwaukee Public Museum:
Outdoor Museums, 1975
Milwaukee Landmarks, 1979*

*ISBN 0-89326-066-5
Library of Congress Catalog Card Number: 81-80378
©Milwaukee Public Museum. All rights reserved.
First edition published 1962; reprinted 1975.
Second edition 1981*

*Milwaukee Public Museum
Publication in History Number Four*

Contents

Foreword

Introduction

Part 1   *Buildings of Wood*

  2 Log and Solid Timber Work
16 The Palisaded Wall
22 Stovewood Construction
30 Half-Timber Work
42 Open Timber Framing
61 The Balloon Frame

Part 2   *Buildings of Brick*

62 Solid Brick Walls
81 Brick Veneer

Part 3   *Buildings of Stone*

 84 Fieldstone Masonry
 97 Cobblestone Work
101 The Gravel Wall
103 Quarried Rock Structures

Foreword

Twenty years ago the Milwaukee Public Museum's *Lore* magazine featured a series of articles by Richard W. E. Perrin, entitled "Historic Wisconsin Buildings - A Survey of Pioneer Architecture 1835-1870." In 1962 these essays were published in booklet form. Going into several printings, it became a highly regarded publication. To assure its further usefulness, a revised and enlarged edition has been prepared to reflect changes wrought by time and circumstance during the past two decades. The author does not intend this to be a comprehensive history of Wisconsin architecture, but rather an introduction to the state's wealth of pioneer structures and building practices, expressing the hope that text and illustrations may suggest further perceptions and lines of thought toward the advancement of historic buildings preservation and restoration in Wisconsin and elsewhere.

Time has not dealt kindly with pioneer buildings; but happily, the record of the past twenty years has not been altogether negative. At the national level a most significant step was taken with the activation of the National Register of Historic Places and attendant legislation designed to implement the endeavors of state historical societies and, as in Wisconsin, the work of the State Review Board for Historic Preservation. Equally significant at the state level, has been the founding and growth of *Old World Wisconsin,* the multi-ethnic outdoor museum near Eagle in Waukesha County. This undertaking, begun in 1964, reached its first major milestone in 1968 with the adoption of a master plan; its second in 1971 with the consummation of a land-lease agreement between the State Historical Society and the Department of Natural Resources; the third, with formal groundbreaking in 1974; and, finally, its dedication and opening to the public in 1976 as a major Bicentennial event.

As to the state's communities, Milwaukee was the first to establish a landmarks commission in 1964. Many other cities and counties have followed suit. While no enabling state legislation has as yet been enacted to give these commissions any real power, they nevertheless are performing a valuable service by identifying landmarks, giving them appropriate recognition and, in general, providing an awareness which might otherwise be lacking altogether.

Some progress has also been made in the private sector, but the restoration and preservation record, both public and private, is not impressive. Actually, more historically important buildings are being destroyed than are being restored. Many are simply surviving, often attended by little more than benign neglect. Of the approximately 150 structures described in *Historic Wisconsin Buildings - A Survey of Pioneer Architecture 1835-1870,* about one-third has been lost or materially altered — and this in a period of barely twenty years.

For this reason, primarily, *Historic Wisconsin Buildings* had to be revised, but the essential thrust remains the same: to reach an ever-widening circle of friends who would share the belief that Wisconsin's historic buildings deserve to be appreciated, recorded in photographs and measured drawings, and the best of them restored and preserved for posterity.

The author, Richard W. E. Perrin, is a Fellow of the American Institute of Architects and Past President of the Wisconsin Academy of Sciences, Arts and Letters. He is also Honorary Curator of History at the Milwaukee Public Museum and has received numerous awards and citations, including the Governor's Award in the Arts. He is the author of several books and many articles on historic preservation, housing and urban planning. Mr. Perrin participated in the original Historic American Buildings Survey of 1933 and has maintained an active voluntary interest in this program up to the present time. He has cataloged more than 700 historic structures in Wisconsin and has completed archival records for many of them. From these extensive studies, as in his earlier writings, informational material and illustrations were carefully selected by Mr. Perrin for presentation in this revised and enlarged edition of *Historic Wisconsin Buildings - A Survey of Pioneer Architecture.*

Kenneth Starr, Director
Milwaukee Public Museum

Introduction

The usual approach to architectural history is in terms of significant cultural movements and resultant styles or identifiable periods. Not nearly so simple is the chronicle of nineteenth century architecture. As we read the record of this culturally, socially and economically divided century with its polarities of human experience, we find no consistent pattern of great architectural expression in classic or romantic mode, except during its first few decades. During these early years, however, Wisconsin was still very primitive and therefore not reflective of trends as they were developing in more populous areas of the country. But then, as the century unfolded, we see many attempts to selectively recombine older styles, with manifestations in Greek Revival, Gothic Revival and other lesser revivals of earlier periods in architectural history.

Additionally, the nineteenth century and even the early twentieth century witnessed such contrasts as primitive frontier conditions in some areas and, concurrently, urban sophistication in others, with little communication between the two. This was particularly evident in Wisconsin. Hewn log structures, for example, had long run their course in southern Wisconsin by 1870, but were still very much in evidence as an important contemporary building type in northern Wisconsin as late as 1920. Moreover, there were chronological lags and overlaps in the style phases themselves. To illustrate, when Greek Revival had already become a thing of the past most everywhere in the country, some excellent work was still being done in this style here in Wisconsin. At the same time buildings were being done in Gothic Revival as well as in numerous varieties of Victorian stylism which for want of a better name are often termed "eclectic."

For this and other related reasons, historical treatment of Wisconsin's pioneer architecture seems to have particular relevancy when regarded according to principal building material and structural concept. These seem to be the more enduring values and, accordingly, three major groups have been delineated: buildings of wood, of brick and of stone. These, in turn, have been subdivided differentially according to building technique.

Prevailing architectural movements and major stylistic manifestations have, of course, been related to these basic structural types, but the emphasis has been placed on the nature of materials, craftsmanship and fundamental design where the most interesting aspects of Wisconsin's pioneer architecture seem to lie.

This presentation is not intended to be an inventory of historic buildings or designated landmarks, since such listings are available elsewhere. Also, while every effort has been made to keep all data current and accurate, it must be remembered that history is not static and new finds and new information are often added to our fund of knowledge, even concerning old and well-known buildings. Finally, it is not possible to provide any assurance that every structure mentioned in the text as being extant is, in fact, still standing, in the same use and under the same ownership. Included buildings are those which seem to best exemplify their particular type. Except for museum buildings which are open during posted hours as well as buildings in obviously public use, privately owned and occupied buildings are not generally open to public view, except by permission or special arrangement.

Richard W. E. Perrin, F.A.I.A.

Part 1 Buildings of Wood

Log and Solid Timber Work

Originally part of the old Northwest Territory and successively part of the Indiana, Illinois and Michigan Territories, Wisconsin became a separate territory in 1836, being admitted to the Union in 1848 as the thirtieth state, with boundaries as they exist today.

While settlements had been established prior to 1836, especially in the orbit of the three pioneer centers of population - Milwaukee, Green Bay and the Southwest - and while the frontier actually continued to push into the northern Wisconsin woodlands until the early part of the present century, a recognizable body of Wisconsin architecture began to emerge in the 1830s which, except for some chronological overlapping that seems to characterize every architectural epoch, eventually became engulfed in the welter of Victorian stylism about the time of the Civil War.

In building their first houses and barns, early settlers of both European and American origin made expedient use of timber which the surrounding forests so bountifully provided. These first buildings were cabins of round or squared logs laid horizontally, with which the settlers coming from the Scandinavian countries, parts of Germany and central Europe generally, were quite familiar. Pennsylvania "Dutch" as well as "Yankees" and "Yorkers" made a fresh introduction of the log house in the new frontier area after its prolific use in some sections of the East a century earlier. Even Belgians and Hollanders with whom log building was no longer a viable tradition — if indeed it ever had been — became experts very quickly, the quality of their work rivaling that of their tradition-trained neighbors.

The log house was precisely what the Wisconsin pioneer needed. It was a house that could be built of material taken from the land as it was cleared, and put together with the same tools as those used in felling the trees. The early log houses were entirely homemade. This is not to say that the task of felling the trees, hewing the logs, hoisting them in place and properly joining them together was a one-man job. On the contrary, it usually took four able-bodied men to erect a log structure, and friends, relatives and neighbors, even if they lived some distance apart, helped each other as needed. Even the women pitched in, and while being spared the heaviest lifting, they could take the reins and guide the oxen as they pulled the logs out of the woods. After the trees were cut and hauled to the site, the logs were squared-up, the bottom notched on the ground and then lifted into position on timber skids. An average log would weigh between 200 and 300 pounds, if tamarack, pine or cedar, and as much as 500 pounds if oak or ash. Almost all varieties of wood were used, except birch which was prone to rot, and such obviously unsuitable kinds as willow and poplar. Unless corner posts were used, which was not very often, by far the trickiest part of the process was the notching and fitting of the corners, usually done by a "corner man" who was particulary dexterous. If this work was not properly done the building would literally fall apart. Types of corner notching differed with people and their place of origin but, basically, there were five popular types of notching: half-notch, steeple or V-notch, saddle-notch, half-dovetail and full-dovetail. One was not necessarily superior to the other, since it was the degree of skill exercised in the shaping and fitting that determined the outcome.

In addition to being his own carpenter and joiner, the early settler had to be his own brickmaker, mason, plasterer and smith. He erected his own homestead and everything connected with it. Perhaps his most useful tool was his ax which he used with great proficiency, from felling a tree to sharpening a branch. He could hold the ax-head in the flat of his hand and dress a piece of wood in the manner of a plane. The handle was marked with notches for measuring timber and, by striking the head with a mallet, a chisel was improvised. Eventu-

Anonymous pioneer mother handling the reins on a mixed ox-horse team — itself an anomaly because of differences in gait and pulling power of the animals. Photograph taken near Oshkosh c. 1880. Courtesy Oshkosh Public Museum.

ally, his tool chest was enlarged to contain a broadax with a curved haft for hewing and squaring the logs and an adze for smooth finish work.

The log house was the universal architectural type of the American frontier, also in Wisconsin. Generally, the pioneer cabins were carefully located with regard to good drainage, correct exposure and a supply of potable water. The earliest log houses were usually one story high with a loft, having a gable roof covered with wooden shakes, bark or even split hollowed logs — the latter being a favorite of Scandinavian settlers who sometimes also chose to lay their roof rafters longitudinally in purlin fashion. First houses would contain only one room which served as kitchen, sitting room and dining room, with sleeping quarters in one corner, sometimes partitioned off by nothing more than a blanket. The loft, approached by ladder, was commonly used as sleeping space for the children. The cellar, if there was one, was simply a hole in the ground, access by trapdoor and a short ladder. The floors of these cabins often were bare ground, tamped and sanded. Rough plank or puncheon floors came later. Puncheons were slabs of hardwood five or six feet long and three to four inches thick, smoothed on the upper side and pegged to stringers laid on the ground. They made a good solid floor which, even if something less than level, was often scoured to the highest degree of cleanliness. As soon as the walls were up, the spaces between the logs were chinked with wooden slats or stone chips to fill the crevices, and these were then covered with clay mixed with straw, followed by lime mortar pargeting. Here again techniques varied considerably. "Yankee" settlers as well as German, Irish, Bohemian and Polish immigrants were inclined to leave ample space between the logs which required substantial chinking — a process, by the way, which had to be repeated every few years as in Wisconsin's climate frost, wind and weather coupled with shrinkage of the logs caused the filling to crumble and fall out, resulting in a leaky and drafty building. Nevertheless, a number of buildings with heavy chinking survived a remarkably long time as, for example, the old Michael Ahner house which had been erected near Saukville in the late 1830s by a German immigrant and which was moved, in part, to the Milwaukee Public Museum as a permanent exhibit. In this very unusual specimen, the chinking is as thick as the adjoining logs, suggesting that the builder was more familiar with masonry construction than with the use of logs. This view is reinforced by the almost complete absence of any kind of corner joining. The logs are simply lapped at these points.

Scandinavians and Finns, on the other hand, fitted their logs and hewn timbers as snugly as they could, and if they used any filling at all it was a strip of fabric laid on top of each log before the next one was placed. Then, the cabin was often allowed to stand for at least a year before door and window openings were cut. The reason for all of this was the Scandinavians and Finns regarded their structures as permanent, whereas most other settlers thought of theirs as temporary or, at least, short-lived — looking forward to the day when they could build themselves a more permanent house of brick or stone masonry. Interestingly, a few of these ostensibly impermanent structures have lasted as long as some of those built far more substantially.

Furniture was as primitive as the buildings. Bedsteads were made of poles fastened to the logs of the wall at a convenient height from the floor. Rough stools and benches fashioned with ax and auger served as chairs. Kitchen utensils were equally simple and often homemade. Mats, quilts and carpets, woven and dyed by the housewife, added a cheerful note of color. Walnut and butternut husks, wild flowers, berries and other products of the earth provided the ingredients for the dyes. Occasionally, a cabin could boast of a deerskin or bearskin rug which likewise was homemade in that the hide was cured and tanned without any professional assistance.

While the log houses of the "Yankees" had their open fireplaces of stone, those of the European settlers who were no longer familiar with the open hearth, had iron stoves. It is known, however, that some of the Germans had their *Kamin*, their *Herd* and their "Dutch oven" in which the fire crackled as merrily as that in their neighbors' fireplaces. Despite their utter simplicity and lack of convenience, there must have been cheer and comfort in these primitive homes of gray logs and bark roofs that marked the clearings, and they were certainly more in harmony with the landscape than many of the more pretentious and spacious houses of a later date.

As the years passed and after they had served their original function, the old log houses were sometimes enlarged and remodeled in currently popular taste. Covering the outside of the log walls with clapboards or vertical boards and battens, while adding nothing to the charm of the house, did serve the practical purpose of protecting the structural fabric and eliminating the inconvenience of periodic re-chinking. The almost universal use of modern composition siding and roofing, unfortunately, did not spare the old log structures. This practice, largely a twentieth century manifestation, did nothing to enhance appearance or longevity. Thus it is that very few of these early log and solid timber structures remain to be seen as originally built. This is particularly true in southern Wisconsin where there must have been thousands 125 years ago. Even in the northern and central sections of the state where settlements occurred late in the nineteenth and early in the twentieth century, really good specimens — original and unaltered — are very hard to find and, when located, are often vacant and deteriorated. Still picturesque, even as ruins, their continuing existence becomes more tenous with each passing winter. To measure and record them, to say nothing of preserving them, is a great challenge.

MICHAEL AHNER log house, built near Saukville in the 1830s, being dismantled for reconstruction as a permanent exhibit at the Milwaukee Public Museum.

Of the small one-room cabins which marked the early pioneer period in Wisconsin, two very good examples may be cited as having survived by falling into sympathetic hands and being creditably restored. They are the John Petty cabin at Aztalan in Jefferson County, and the Goodrich cabin in Milton, Rock County. Both of these cabins were built by "Yankees" in the late 1830s and are typical of the smaller variety built by pioneers coming from New England. Characteristically, both the Petty and the Goodrich cabins were provided with massive split rock chimneys situated on the end wall and, of course, accommodating a large open fireplace on the inside.

PETTY CABIN, Aztalan, south elevation.

TURCK-SCHOTTLER HOUSE near Kirchhayn, now in Old World Wisconsin, viewed from southwest.

One of the best and completely unspoiled specimens of early log architecture of German provenance is the Fred Schottler home which until very recently stood in the Town of Germantown, Washington County. Very fortunately, this excellent building was one of the first to be acquired, dismantled, transported and rebuilt in *Old World Wisconsin,* the outdoor ethnographic museum near Eagle in Waukesha County, now being developed by the State Historical Society of Wisconsin in cooperation with the Department of Natural Resources of the State of Wisconsin. This house, believed to have been built by Christian Turck in the early 1840s is of the "salt box" type. The logs are cedar and were probably felled in the swamp that adjoined the original site. Some of the floor timbers are of oak and ash, and a longitudinal summer-beam runs through the center of the house at both floor levels. The spaces between the floor beams resting on the summer-beams were filled with clay mixed with rye straw. A cantilevered hood extends across the entire south front and the long slope of the roof faces north, with little wall exposure below, to protect the house from winter winds. This excellent specimen of log construction, and generally recognized as such, would certainly not have survived except for the fortuitous decision to acquire it, move it to *Old World Wisconsin,* and there to properly restore it.

GOODRICH CABIN, *Milton, viewed from northwest.*

JOHN BERGEN HOUSE, town of Norway. Northwest elevation, destroyed by vandals.

KETOLA HOUSE, town of Oulu. Original location, viewed from southwest.

Not so fortunate, to cite but one example, was the John Bergen house in the Town of Norway, Racine County. The loss of this house is particularly poignant because it was one of the last surviving examples of a Norwegian "gallery" house, so-called because of a two-story gallery or *svalgang* which extended across the entire front of the house and by which access was gained to both first and second story rooms. This type of design reaches back many centuries into Scandinavian building tradition. The logs were oak, all carefully hewn and fitted. Most of the trim was pine and the doors were raised-panel made of black walnut, equipped with hand-wrought iron hinges and latches. Built in 1843 by Osten Meland, a Norwegian immigrant, the house was burned to the ground in 1968 by vandals unknown. It is unfortunate that *Old World Wisconsin* had not progressed sufficiently at the time to undertake removal and restoration of this house, but because of its rarity as to type, accurate measurements were taken by the writer shortly before its destruction. If ever it is decided to reproduce in facsimile a building such as this and no longer extant anywhere, enough information exists to thus reproduce the John Bergen house.

Old World Wisconsin has become the repository for a number of other interesting log and solid timber buildings. Following the concept of clustering structures according to national or ethnic orgins of the original owners or builders, one of the first groups to be completed is the Finnish farmstead comprising dwelling, stock-barn, hay-barn, sauna and ancillary buildings. The house is a particularly important specimen. It was built in three stages, between 1894 and 1900, by an early Finnish settler named Ketola — later Anglicized to Getto — in Oulu Township, Bayfield County. It is a typical Finnish, one-story, hewn timber structure, following the ancient Nordic "hearth-house" pattern with three rooms in a row. The size of these rooms is rooted in tradition and, to some extent, determined by the length of appropriate timber available in this already cut-over land. Despite its well-maintained condition, the isolated location and other factors militated against any assurance that the Ketola house would survive on site. At any rate, removal to the outdoor museum guaranteed its restoration and survival in perpetuity.

Several other important early log and timber structures have been saved by moving them to smaller outdoor museums such as the Ozaukee County Pioneer Village near Waubeka. Among these is the Hashek barn which was originally situated near Myra in Washington County. Built of squared and carefully fitted cedar logs, the barn is attributed to an early Bohemian settler of the area. Its exact date is not known but judging from the condition of the logs and other factors this barn may have been built as early as 1855. Similar to a number of houses of this period, the Hashek barn originally had a "salt box" profile. Careful study of these old structures reveals interesting variations in treatment arising from traditions brought along by the settlers or simply personal preferences of the builders. The Hashek barn has no filling or chinking between the logs in order to allow a free movement of air though the hay-mow and granary, but still protecting the contents from the elements.

As a completely private endeavor involving the relocation and restoration of a single log structure, the old Vauk house, also known as Dallmann house, is quite outstanding. Abandoned and lacking maintenance after the last occupant died, the building was acquired by the Historical Society of Trinity Lutheran Church of Freistadt, Ozaukee County, and moved to the grounds of the church. Freistadt is the oldest German settlement in Wisconsin, founded in 1839 by Pomeranian immigrants from the old Kingdom of Prussia. The Dallmann house was originally located in Washington County, a few miles northwest of Freistadt and had been built by Peter Vauk around 1850. A well-built structure of massive oak logs with a fieldstone addition built about 1870, this too was a "salt box" house originally. Unfortunately, the addition was not included in the restoration.

HASHEK BARN near Myra, now in Ozaukee County Pioneer Village, viewed from southeast.

VAUK HOUSE viewed from east as relocated on grounds of Trinity Lutheran Church at Freistadt.

MEIDENBAUER HOUSE, New Berlin seen from southwest, and detail of entrance and timberwork.

There are no longer any concentrations of log and solid hewn timber buildings anywhere in the state, but diligent scanning will still disclose scattered specimens of great significance. The prospect of losing these buildings must always be seriously considered, making the preservation of those that remain all the more imperative.

In this context, at least four houses of this type in widely separated parts of the state may be cited as examples. Perhaps the oldest of these is the Meidenbauer house in New Berlin, Waukesha County. Apparently, this house and two dependent buildings had been built by Francis Shore prior to 1848 when the farm was bought by John Konrad Meidenbauer, a Bavarian immigrant, for the sum of $800.00. The purchase price included land, buildings and crops already planted. Thrown into the bargain were 4 pigs, 4 sheep, 12 chickens and 50 heads of cabbage. The house, still standing, was built of hewn oak logs with full dovetailed corners. It is an excellent example of pioneer architecture in southeastern Wisconsin.

Tucked into the hills of Iowa County, very scenically situated, is the Weissenfluh house, believed to date back to 1850 or earlier. Also built of oak logs, the hewing and joining are unique in that the logs were slightly rounded at the top and a very tight joint achieved with a modified steeple notch. This house with its picturesque setting is a beautiful specimen meriting preservation if at all possible.

Moving up into the northwestern part of the state, mention deserves to be made of the old Jonas Ojala house in the Town of Oulu, Bayfield County, and in the northeast, the Bavry house near Carlsville, Door County. The Ojala house was built around 1900 by a lay preacher of the Finnish Apostolic Lutheran Church, Jonas Ojala, with typical Finnish treatment of full hewn timber. Additionally, the premises include an early type of root cellar and the relic of a sauna structure with the original stone fireplace. The Bavry house was built in 1888 by a Norwegian immigrant, Jacob Baevre, and is characteristic of the early Norwegian work in this area. Both the Ojala and Bavry houses are in seriously deteriorated condition, but not completely beyond recall if means and motivation could be found.

JONAS OJALA HOUSE, town of Oulu, viewed from southwest.

BAVRY HOUSE near Carlsville, west elevation.

WEISSENFLUH HOUSE, near Ridgeway. Viewed from southeast.

CHIVIOK BARN near Phillips, west elevation.

LAMMI BARN near Maple, viewed from southeast.

Perhaps the most curiously photogenic log barn in Wisconsin is the fourteen-sided structure on the Jerome Chiviok place, east of Phillips in Price County. Situated on Musser Flowage of the Big Elk River, and secluded even now, this most unusual barn is an almost unbelievable achievement, considering the date of its construction around 1895 when this part of Wisconsin was still very wild and sparsely populated timber country. Using slightly squared pine logs the builder, thought to have been Henry Rademacher, used a framing and joining technique strongly suggesting East German provenance. When last examined this building, also, appeared ruinous but not necessarily beyond repair. May the hope be expressed that it has survived and that it will be restored and preserved.

It is interesting to note that log barns seem to have survived more often than houses, probably because they remained functional and useful in the face of changing fashion. Thus, it is possible to identify a whole series of barns of good design and excellent quality, particularly in the Kewaunee and Door County areas where, for example, a substantial number of Belgian barns remain to be seen. Some of the best of these are located in Brussels and Gardner Township of Door County. Barns of various kinds also figure prominently in areas settled by the Finns in the late nineteenth and twentieth centuries. Thus Douglas and Bayfield Counties provide a number of excellent examples such as the Lammi and Koivu cattle barns and the Beck hay barn — all near Maple in Douglas County. In terms of auxiliary buildings, the Finnish saunas figure very prominently and a few early specimens, built of logs, are still to be seen.

KOIVU BARN near Maple. Detail of roof and treatment of timberwork.

BECK HAYBARN near Maple, seen from southeast.

DAVIDSON WINDMILL, town of Lakeside. Viewed from northeast.

The only structure of its kind remaining in the state is the Davidson windmill on Amnicon Creek in Lakeside Township, Douglas County. This hewn log structure, built around 1900, is a carry-over into modern times of a rural Finnish tradition going back into centuries of the past. Its revolving turret, also made of hewn timbers, is equipped with an eight-armed wheel, characteristically Finnish in every way. While no longer functioning as a grist mill, it remains a cherished landmark because of continuing concern by local people.

ABANDONED SAUNA, surviving example of popular structure in the vicinity of Maple.

HAUGE NORWEGIAN EVANGELICAL LUTHERAN CHURCH, near Daleyville. View from church cemetery looking west.

HAUGE NORWEGIAN EVANGELICAL LUTHERAN CHURCH, near Daleyville. Interior view of pulpit and chancel.

Similarly, a few log churches have managed to survive, even though they are no longer in active use. Sentimental attachment is the usual motivation for the preservation of such buildings and which, happily, has resulted in saving at least two such structures. One of these is the Hauge Norwegian Evangelical Lutheran Church, a few miles south of Mt. Horeb near Daleyville in Dane County. While the exterior was eventually clapboarded, the interior discloses the original treatment which consisted of lime plaster applied directly to the logs, resulting in a very pleasant texture. This church was built in 1852 and used for many years. But, finally standing vacant, its restoration was achieved by a small group of concerned people who have opened the church to the public as a small museum of Norwegian Lutheransim in Wisconsin. It is a tiny structure measuring only about 18 by 18 feet inside. Pulpit and altar are combined in the old Norwegian fashion, and the small, straight-backed pews, obviously homemade, are unfinished pine.

Another log church owing its rescue to interested friends and descendants of early church members is St. Wenceslaus Roman Catholic Church, two miles east of Waterloo in Jefferson County. Built about 1850 by German speaking Bohemian settlers, the walls of this church are solid tamarack log construction. The outside walls were sheathed with vertical boards and battens, but it is surmised that this treatment was added around 1870 when this type of surfacing enjoyed considerable popularity. The inside of this church, like the Hauge Church, was finished with a coat of lime plaster applied directly to the logs and left in the original natural off-white color. Still in place, the original pews cut from pine boards are defintely Baroque in concept, and together with the altar, old heating-stove and appurtenances of all kinds, combine to make St. Wenceslaus an exceptionally authentic and unspoiled specimen of pioneer church architecture.

ST. WENCESLAUS ROMAN CATHOLIC CHURCH, near Waterloo, viewed from southeast.

ST. WENCESLAUS ROMAN CATHOLIC CHURCH, near Waterloo. Interior view looking west toward chancel and altar.

PLANK-SCHULER HOUSE, Brillion. Palisaded structure in process of being dismantled, viewed from southwest.

The Palisaded Wall

Building with closely set vertical logs or hewn timbers was known throughout Europe since Neolithic times and continued in use to some extent well into the nineteenth century, but it remained for the French in America to employ palisaded construction most extensively. *Poteaux en terre* was the earliest method used by French settlers in Canada, the Great Lakes region and up and down the Mississippi River valley. The technique was simple in that closely spaced vertical posts were simply set into a trench, then back-filled and well tamped for rigidity. The interstices, often as wide or wider than the post itself, were generally filled with mud and straw and pargeted with lime mortar. If the stakes were sharpened and driven into the ground, but treated the same otherwise, the construction was called *pieux en terre*. Somewhat later, by way of refinement and probably in the interest of better alignment and greater stability, the vertical members were placed upon, and usually tenoned into a horizontal timber sill. This was termed *poteaux sur sole*.

Curiously, and in view of the not inconsiderable influence of the French in early Wisconsin affairs, no significant examples of their palisaded walls have been turned up thus far — not even in the Green Bay area where many other types of pioneer French construction are known to have existed. Actually, the most important specimens of palisaded work found so far have been houses and barns of German, Bohemian, Swedish and Finnish provenance. Without exception, they appear to be *poteaux en sole* of some sort, but whether they were patterned after any respective prototypes or adapted from French work extant at one time but now extinct, is open to conjecture.

Of the German work the most notable discovery thus far is the palisaded timber house built in 1866 by Henry Plank in Brillion, Calumet County. Pine and cedar timbers were hewn to a uniform thickness of seven inches, set upright upon and mortised into hewn timber girders, and capped at the top with a timber plate. The gaps between the vertical timbers were well chinked with clay and chopped straw. The floor joist, interior studs and roof rafters were not hewn but rough sawn. Foundation walls were fieldstone rubble masonry. The outside of the house was clapboarded and the inside was lathed and plastered. The last and long-time owner-occupant was Max Schuler, and in 1968 the house was razed, but not before measurements were taken and arrangements made to have the structural components transported to *Old World Wisconsin* where they may eventually be reconstituted to illustrate the palisade method of wall building.

If, in the context of the American cultural amalgam, national or ethnic origins of the builders can confer ethnicity upon the buildings, then the Blashka and Vomastic houses must be regarded as Slavic. Still, there is no appreciable difference in the way these palisaded walls were built and, therefore, could just as easily be considered as German as the Plank house or, for that matter, French *poteaux sur sole* in every respect.

The Blashka house is located north of Maribel, in Cooperstown Township, Manitowoc County. The plan is T-shaped and only the kitchen wing is palisaded construction, the main part being conventional, horizontal hewn-timber work which, incidentally contains cedar logs exceeding 26″ caliper. The kitchen wing may well have been an addition, but the main part of the house is believed to have been built around 1880. When last seen the house was vacant and in poor condition but picturesque nevertheless. Ironically, it is only when buildings are falling apart or being torn down that an opportunity is afforded to examine and study the components in order to determine how and why they were built the way they were.

PLANK-SCHULER HOUSE, Brillion. Detail of palisaded wall construction.

BLASHKA HOUSE near Maribel, southwest elevation.

VOMASTIC HOUSE, town of Waukechon, south elevation.

REZEK PALISADED BARN near Maribel, northeast elevation.

The Vomastic house also has a T-plan, but here the treatment is reversed in that the main part has palisaded walls and the wing is built of horizontal timbers. The walls were furred and clapboarded on the outside, lathed and plastered on the inside. This house, located in Waukechon Township of Shawano County, appears to have been built around 1890. It, too, is vacant and abandoned but still sufficiently sound, structurally, to suggest preservation and restoration possibilities.

Barns were also built with palisaded walls and in the Slavic category, the poultry barn on the Leo Rezek place comes to mind as one of the best specimens. This barn is located near Maribel and was built by Anton Rezek in 1901. The Rezek family was Bohemian but it is not known whether the use of vertical timbers was an ethnic tradition or just "picked-up" along the way. Turn of the century examples are about the latest palisaded structures to be found in Wisconsin.

Somewhat more readily identifiable as to their ethnicity are the palisaded structures of the Finns and Scandinavians generally. Excellent examples, although never plentiful, may still be seen in Douglas County, especially in the Town of Maple. While there are differences in plan and elevation, the palisading shows much similarity in that the timbers were not hewn any more than they had to be. Stripped of their bark, the logs were flattened just sufficiently along the sides to permit a reasonably snug fit when they were positioned upright. Elaborate chinking of wide interstices, so much favored by other ethnic groups, was studiously avoided by Finns and Swedes, and greater reliance was placed on careful edging and fitting of timbers whether laid horizontally or made to stand upright.

That palisaded wall construction survived in the Nordic building tradition brought to Wisconsin by Scandinavian settlers is understandable, recalling that such vertical timbering with its almost unbelievably long ancestry was still viable in the nineteenth century. Ranking among the greatest architectural achievements of the early Middle Ages are the palisaded stave churches — the *Stavkirker* — found throughout Scandinavia, in England and wherever Viking influence extended. These churches were actually pole structures with palisaded infilling, and reached their peak of excellence in the 11th and 12th century. Reflecting a high degree of artistic perception and technical skill, these churches were built by the same order of craftsmen who, several centuries earlier, had constructed the now famous burial ships of Gokstad and Oseberg — all eloquent testimonials to a fine understanding of material and functional form, not always fully achieved even in the great architecture, both civil and naval, of any age. Interestingly, the burial chambers aboard the Gokstad and Oseberg ships were also palisaded construction.

Though little more than vestigial, and certainly very limited in distribution, the palisaded walls of Wisconsin's Scandinavian buildings nevertheless recall an important structural concept deeply rooted in Nordic antiquity.

One of the more interesting Swedish type barns is on the Pearson farm in the vicinity of Cloverland. It is a steep gambrel roofed structure flanked by a flat roofed wing on either side, and it is these wings that were built with palisaded walls. Of the Finnish variety, at least three barns may be cited as outstanding examples of palisaded construction. They are, as locally identified, the Penttila barn and the Hakala barn in the Town of Maple, Douglas County, and the Ruokenen barn in the same area. All of them were built around the turn of the century. Like the Swedish Pearson barn,

PEARSON BARN near Maple, viewed from southeast.

PENTTILA BARN near Maple, viewed from southwest.

the Finnish Penttila barn has a steep gambrel roof but no side wings. The similarity in design which appears to be Swedish may be accounted for by remembering that, as in many other relationships, Finland came into the orbit of Swedish influence for six and a half centuries when it was an integral part of the Kingdom of Sweden. Aside of the full palisaded walls, the Penttila barn has rare and unusual roof covering in the form of lapped boards, also laid vertically rather than horizontally. This type of roof was rather common in the old country but not much favored in Wisconsin — long cedar shakes and even bark being the preferred material.

The Ruokenen barn is a somewhat larger structure with an easier slope to its gambrel roof which is clad with hand-rived cedar shingles. These shingles are two feet long, lapped about a foot and showing one foot to the weather. The palisaded walls of this barn are extremely well made, having survived three-quarters of a century without any siding, sheathing or outside covering of any kind.

The Hakala barn is a so-called "long" barn because of its relatively great length and the way it was compartmented. The walls are palisaded and the roof is a simple gable of average slope but also covered with long cedar shingles. This barn is still in relatively good condition, as are the others, but to assume that any of them will survive indefinitely would be a mistake. They are no longer in use but remain valuable historic assets nevertheless. Their preservation deserves high priority.

RUOKONEN BARN near Maple, detail of palisaded wall.

RUOKONEN BARN near Maple, viewed from northwest.

HAKALA LONG BARN near Maple, viewed from southeast.

MECIKALSKI BOARDING HOUSE AND SALOON, Lennox, south elevation.

Stovewood Construction

A further important variant of solid timber work is the so-called stovewood wall, also referred to as cordwood or stackwood construction — particularly in Canada where it continues to be used even today. It appears to be the only type of log construction that does not have any clear-cut antecedents in European building history. Its origins can only be traced to Canada where itinerant lumberjacks erected such structures in their logging camps early in the nineteenth century. While scattered examples have been located throughout the United States, Wisconsin seems to have an exceptional concentration. First employed by settlers from New England and New York, stovewood construction was picked up by Germans, Poles and Scandinavians and used in the northeasterly part of the state as recently as the first decade of the present century.

Basically, there are two varieties of stovewood construction. The first type is a hewn timber, braced frame in which stovewood has been used as nogging in the panels, in manner similar to brick, rubble or wattle-and-daub filler, thus resulting in a form of half-timber work. The timbers, usually seven to eight inches in thickness, determined the length of the stovewood pieces which were flush with the timbers on both sides. These pieces of stovewood were simply sticks of wood prepared from the limbs and trunks of trees, cut to the desired length and split to appropriate size if required. Thereupon, they were laid close together, at right angle to the timber members of the frame, packed tightly and solidly bedded in lime mortar. Viewed head-on such a wall looked very much like a well stacked pile of stovewood, or cordwood, from which the name derives. After erection of the walls, with the roof also in place, they were sometimes given a skim coat of lime plaster and, more often than not, were shingled, clapboarded or clad with vertical boards on the outside. The interiors of barns and other purely utilitarian buildings were generally plastered just like the outside. House interiors were often conventionally lathed and plastered.

After heavy timber framing gave way to lighter construction techniques employing mostly sawn two-inch members, stovewood filler continued to be used between the studs, presumably for insulation purposes.

The second type of stovewood wall is massive, having been built without any kind of frame. By virtue of its mass, ranging from fourteen to twenty inches in thickness, such a wall was completely self-supporting. Corners were usually formed with squared timber blocks similar to cut-stone quoins in rubble masonry walls. Massive stovewood walls were also plastered, optionally, both inside and outside but in most instances were not clapboarded or sheathed on the outside.

The first stovewood structure of which there is any record in Wisconsin annals was built in 1848 near Williams Bay in Walworth County by David Williams of New York state and a lineal descendant of Roger Williams, founder of Rhode Island. This house had walls of the massive stovewood type, made entirely of oak. It may safely be surmised that there were many similarly built structures in southern Wisconsin during the early years but as with so many other historic types, they were swept away by advancing waves of population. But, at least to some extent, they were carried forward with the frontier as it moved into the northern sections of the state.

As far as can be determined, virtually all of the surviving stovewood buildings lie north of the forty-fourth parallel. Those that are situated east of Green Bay and, therefore, primarily in Door County, are almost invariably of the half-timber variety and the wood is usually cedar or a conifer of some kind. The buildings west of the Bay and, therefore, on the mainland are nearly always of the massive type, with hardwoods being used about as often as softwoods, most likely on the basis of what was most readily available.

MECIKALSKI BOARDING HOUSE AND SALOON, Lennox. Detail at south elevation showing stovewood technique.

WILCOX BARN near Angelica. Detail of stovewood construction.

MASTEY BARN near Angelica, seen from southwest.

Massive stovewood walls were sometimes raised two stories in height. One of the most impressive examples of this type still in existence, though in poor condition, is the Mecikalski building in Lennox, Oneida County. It was built by Edwin Wolfgram about 1895 and for many years was a boarding house and saloon, patronized by lumberjacks and sawmill hands. The walls of this building are eighteen inches thick and exceptionally large cedar logs up to sixteen inches in diameter were used and interspersed with others ranging from four to eight inch caliper. The front and back walls had clapboarding but the condition of the side walls suggests that they may always have been exposed.

Most of the surviving massive stovewood structures are barns and farm buildings rather than dwellings, although one of them, on the

CORNELIUS BARN near Shawano, viewed from southwest.

ISON STOVEWOOD BARN near Crandon. Detail of corner showing hewn-timber quoins.

WENDELL ISON BARN near Crandon. East elevation showing stovewood foundation.

Wilcox farm near Angelica, is believed to have been a house originally and converted to a stock barn later on. This structure is only partly stovewood, the remainder being fieldstone rubble masonry. Moreover, the stovewood technique here employed is not typical in that the timbers consist of alternating rows of horizontal pieces, but massive nevertheless. There are several other stovewood barns of great interest in the Angelica-Pulaski-Krakow area of Shawano County which, very probably, are the work of early Polish settlers. One of these is the Mastey barn, built with something of a "saltbox" profile with the north end of the roof being hipped. The massive stovewood wall contains some unusually large chunks, mostly hardwood, used in the full round or halved with just enough splits worked in to fill the voids. The timber quoins are also extremely heavy, giving the whole structure a very substantial appearance. Near Shawano itself, a rather large barn is located on the Dale Cornelius farm. While in other respects a typical old-style stock barn, the lower part of the building, so often built of fieldstone masonry, is stovewood in this instance. The superstructure is open timber framing, and one section of the barn is made of horizontal logs, said to date back to the 1870s. Another interesting dairy barn with massive stovewood foundation walls is located on the Wendell Ison farm near Crandon. It has been kept in good condition, attesting that even construction such as stovewood, if properly maintained, will retain its stability and utility almost indefinitely.

Two prime specimens of stovewood, located in Lena, Oconto County, were recently

LA PLANT BARN near Lena, viewed from southwest.

destroyed. They were classic examples of craftsmanship but of subsequent neglect as well. With minimum care these buildings could have survived. Unfortunately, there are few buildings of this type still to be seen in this area, although there is one directly east of Lena about five miles which has been kept in good repair. It was originally a small barn, believed to have been built by an early settler named La Plant and is located in an area in which a number of pioneer French families made their homes.

In the other major category of stovewood construction, half-timber with stovewood nogging, the best and comparatively frequent survivals are located in Door County. Their builders, as far as can be determined, were generally German, Scandinavian and, possibly, Bohemain. Barns were often built entirely of stovewood but houses often had only stovewood wings attached to earlier houses built of conventional horizontal log construction. Two such specimens of considerable importance are located across the road from each other on Highway 57 in Baileys Harbor Township, southeast of Ephraim. The first of these, on the east side of the road, consists of a log house built in 1860 and a stovewood wing added in 1898. This house was the work of August Dorn, one of the earliest German settlers to come to the area. He also built a stovewood barn and smokehouse. The latter remains, as does the dwelling, but the barn was destroyed in a windstorm. However, none of these buildings would have survived but for the efforts of the present owners, Mr. and Mrs. Marvin Corman, who restored and renovated the buildings.

DORN HOUSE, town of Baileys Harbor. Interior view of living room showing treatment of stovewood restoration.

DORN HOUSE, town of Baileys Harbor. Viewed from northeast while in process of being restored.

ZACHOW HOUSE, town of Baileys Harbor. Interior showing stovewood before restoration.

ZACHOW HOUSE, town of Baileys Harbor. Detail of stovewood construction under shingles.

ZACHOW HOUSE, town of Baileys Harbor. East elevation before restoration.

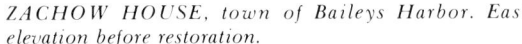

HERMANN-BRAUN BARN near Baileys Harbor, viewed from west.

The house across the road to the west was also built by August Dorn, but for his daughter who had married William Zachow and subsequently raised ten children in this house. Again, the main part of the house, built around 1880, is of horizontal log construction and a stovewood kitchen wing was added in 1909. This house had reached a point of almost irretrievable disrepair, but fortunately was acquired by John Kahlert and creditably restored. Unfortunately, a stovewood granary building on the premises could not be salvaged.

One of the most recent restoration efforts being undertaken in the Baileys Harbor area is the old Herrmann barn under the direction of Louis Braun who recently acquired the premises. This barn is one of the most significant stovewood structures in Door County and its restoration is a most encouraging development.

The popularity of stovewood construction, except for the very early work in the southern part of the state, seems to have spanned only two decades, roughly 1895 to 1915. As with all pioneer architecture, each passing year marks the disappearance of yet another irreplaceable structure. Part of this process is inevitable but for the sake of posterity at least some part of the historic architectural legacy should be preserved.

ROI-PORLIER-TANK HOUSE, Green Bay. Seen from west prior to relocation in Heritage Hill State Park.

Half-Timber Work

By standard definition, half-timber work is a kind of wall construction in which heavy timbers — mortised, tenoned and pegged together — are composed into a frame, and the open spaces, or panels, filled with masonry of some kind which might be kiln-fired brick, air dried brick, rubble stone masonry, or a clay and straw mixture applied to wooden staves or a network of branches and twigs known as wattle-and-daub. A wall of this sort had the advantage of providing a measure of fire resistance and vermin proofing, thermal insulation and, in some instances, additional structural stability.

Half-timber work, in a number of varieties, was extremely popular in mediaeval Europe, particularly England, France and Germany. Due to a dwindling supply of timber, coupled with the advisability of building more completely fire-resistive buildings in an age of almost continuous warfare, half-timber work was gradually phased out in favor of solid masonry construction. However, in sparsely settled rural areas such as eastern Germany, half-timber work remained popular well into the nineteenth century.

English Pilgrims brought the half-timber house to America early in the seventeenth century, and Frenchmen built their own variety in all parts of New France. There were, of course, regional and other differences brought about be requirements of climate, utility and availability of material but, in the main, the buildings in the colonies reflected national origins. Similarly, Germans of various kinds built half-timber houses wherever they established themselves in the late seventeenth century. To the extent that this type of building remained viable in the homeland, immigrants continued to use it in the New World as their status and financial situation permitted. This is why later German work, being of more recent date, has survived more frequently than that of the French, for example, which may only be found as isolated specimens. Except for a few total facsimile restorations, early English and German colonial work may, for all practical purposes, be considered extinct.

In Wisconsin, because of the high percentage of East German immigrants settling in the state during the nineteenth century, there was a correspondingly high incidence of half-timber construction during that period. A fair number of these buildings has survived although not too frequently in unaltered condition. For the first German arrivals, as with other ethnic groups, the log house provided their only shelter, but when the first and hardest part of pioneering was done some of the more customary amenities followed, and in what they considered as a permanent house to replace the log cabin, they frequently opted for a half-timber structure. In German, half-timber work is called *Fachwerkbau* and sometimes, in Wisconsin German vernacular, it was known as *deutscher Verband*.

Still, the oldest half-timber building in Wisconsin is not German but French. This is the Roi-Porlier-Tank Cottage in Green Bay, which is also the state's oldest house of any kind. The main part of the house was built in 1776 by or for Joseph Roi, a French fur trader, who had acquired and cleared a few acres of land in the French settlement of La Baye, the early name for Green Bay. Two wings were added to the house at a later date but the central part, which originally contained nine rooms, had walls of half-timber which may still be seen. The spaces between the upright timbers have vertical tree branches arranged so that smaller branches could be woven in horizontally. Then this network of branches was thoroughly plastered and back-plastered with a mixture of clay, lime, straw and leaves which, when dry, became a hard, solid mass. While probably not altogether orthodox in the way it was done, this treatment is nevertheless identifiable as French *bousillage*. The Roi-Porlier-Tank house was restored a number of years ago, was moved several times and finally placed in Green Bay's Heritage Hill State Park, a 43 acre tract overlooking the Fox River and which eventually will accomodate a substantial number of relocated historic structures.

Of the mid-nineteenth century German half-timber buildings in Wisconsin, one of the most interesting is the Langholff house near Watertown, Dodge County. The walls of this house are a good example of the early form of nogging consisting of wood staves let into the horizontal framing timbers, covered with a mixture of straw and mud, pargetted with plaster. This is very much like *bousillage*, except that the French generally used horizontal staves let into the vertical timbers, largely because French half-timber work, *batisse en cloisonnage*, consisted essentially of vertical timbers with very little by way of diagonal bracing and virtually no horizontal girts. There is a German equivalent to this known as *Staenderbau*, but it is an older form, involving the use of much more timber, which gave way to *Rahmenbau*, the braced frame, and which characterizes virtually all Wisconsin half-timber work of German provenance. As the Langholff house began to deteriorate, some of the mud and straw filling began to fall away

LANGHOLFF HOUSE near Watertown, viewed from southeast.

from the staves and was replaced with nogging of handmade, kiln-fired brick. Built around 1848, this building is one of the very few half-timber structures known to have accomodated both dwelling and cattle barn under one roof. A central hall separated the living quarters from the barn and at the end of the hall was situated a vaulted, brick walk-in compartment which was used for the smoking of meat and may also have incorporated a bake-oven. In Germany such a facility was known as *schwarze Kueche* and occured with some regularity, but in Wisconsin it was a rarity. The cattle barn part of the Langholff building had a hay loft and granary on the upper level and the dwelling part had the bedrooms on this same level. The other animals — horses, sheep, pigs and poultry — were sheltered in separate buildings. It is surmised that the Langholff house was built by Friedrich Kliese, an early settler who came from the Prussian province of Silesia, although the place was subsequently owned by the Scholz family for more than seventy years. While definitely *Rahmenbau*, the Langholff house and barn combination nevertheless discloses middle German characteristics not generally associated with Wisconsin half-timber structures which are predominantly of northern and eastern German provenance. The plan, the fairly steep roof, the fenestration and other features bear out this presumption. Another house with similar characteristics is the old Schoenicke place, near Lebanon, now in ruins. In this building unusually heavy timbers were used and the brick, made on the site, had an exceptionally pleasant vermilion shade and good texture. Although perhaps incapable of restoration, it was possible to take measurements and photographs of this house for the record and for the purpose of providing a basis should facsimile reproduction ever be desired for museological use.

Wisconsin German half-timber work was generally white oak, although some buildings such as the Rusch house and the Krause house near Kirchayn in Jackson Township, Washington County, were built of cedar and tamarack taken from nearby swamps. While there were some distinct differences in framing technique, a heavy squared timber still was generally laid close to the ground upon a fieldstone foundation and the floor beams were tenoned into it. At the corners, and near the center, posts were erected extending the full height to the rafter plate. The end panels were braced diagonally. Intermediate posts, usually one story high, were then placed to frame openings for windows and doors. At the second floor level, a girt was tenoned to mortises in the posts, and carrying all around the house, the floor beams were notched into the girt. The second floor walls were framed like those below, topped by a timber plate into which the rafters were heeled. Rafters were frequently poles of tamarack, with one side flattened only enough to secure the roof boards. In other instances, the rafters were as carefully hewn and fitted as the rest of the timber frame. No nails were used to hold the pieces together since all joints were mortised and tenoned and secured with tapered hardwood pegs. Each major timber was carefully marked with a Roman Numeral chiseled into its exposed flank to identify its relative position in the frame. A thin coat of lime plaster was frequently troweled over the entire wall. Roof boards were often 12 to 20 inches wide and covered with handmade wooden shingles. In a few instances it has been satisfactorily documented that thatched roofs were used as had been the custom in Europe for many centuries.

Somewhat similar to the Rusch and Krause houses in several important respects is the Schulz-Zirbel house which until very recently stood on a pioneer farmstead near Iron Ridge

RUSCH HOUSE near Kirchhayn, viewed from southeast.

KRAUSE HOUSE near Kirchhayn, south elevation.

in Dodge County. It is distinguished primarily because of its prominent *schwarze Kueche* located in the center of the house with a tapered brick hood and chimney extending up and through the roof. This outstanding specimen of half-timber architecture was acquired for *Old World Wisconsin* and is now being restored at that location. Like most half-timber structures of this *genre,* it was built during the middle years of the nineteenth century.

Also relocated in *Old World Wisconsin* and now fully restored is the old Koepsel house which came from Jackson Township in Washington County. It is one of the most handsome German half-timber houses still in existence. Built somewhat later than most of its kind, the documented date appears to be 1860. The house is two stories high with a full loft which was used as a traditional *Trockenboden*

SCHULZ-ZIRBEL HOUSE near Iron Ridge. Pyramidal smoke-chamber of black kitchen viewed from loft.

SCHULZ-ZIRBEL HOUSE near Iron Ridge, now in Old World Wisconsin, viewed from northwest.

but also, it seems, as sleeping quarters for the hired men. The plan is symmetrical with a central hall and handsome staircase. A vestigial *schwarze Kueche* is a smoke chamber contained in a flared portion of the chimney on the second floor — not large enough to be entered but only sufficient for hanging meats and sausages to be smoked, The timber is white oak and the brick apparently was made on the site or nearby, since the characteristic cream and flesh tones are definite hallmarks of local clay. The kitchen floor was paved with some of the same brick, although the other floors are covered with random width softwood boards.

An early carpenter and joiner in the Kirchhayn area was Gottlieb Krueger. The half-timber house he built for himself on what later became the Arthur Miske farm dates back to 1848. In size it measures 26 by 44 feet and is also symmetrical in plan, with a central hall running through the house. The timbers are oak and the panels between them are filled with unusual handmade, air-dried bricks containing clay, straw and pea gravel — literally a form of adobe. These bricks are oversized, 5 by 4 by 10½ inches, and were laid in mud mortar. The Krueger house is still covered with oak clapboards, but it is not known with any certainty whether this treatment was original or a later addition. The condition of the clapboards suggests many years of weathering and it may therefore be surmised that when the mud brick and plaster pargeting were found not to withstand the extremes of temperature too well, clapboarding was applied.

KOEPSEL HOUSE, *town of Jackson, Washington County, now in Old World Wisconsin, northeast elevation.*

KRUEGER HOUSE *near Kirchhayn, viewed from southwest.*

BRAEMER HOUSE near Hustisford. Old photograph taken around 1890, showing original half-timber work. Photo courtesy of Mr. Obed Braemer.

As a rule, *Fachwerk* buildings did not have fireplaces, as the Germans, unlike their Irish, English and Yankee neighbors, preferred to heat their houses with stoves; but there were some notable exceptions. For example, the Braemer house, between Hustisford and Woodland, Dodge County was definitely known to have a large open *Kamin* in the combination kitchen and living room. Still to be seen are the 9 inch octagonal tiles used in the fireplace and adjoining floors. They are of the same mellow vermillion color as the Hustisford brick used in the nogging of this *Fachwerk* building. Unfortunately, however, no *Kamin* seems to have survived intact, so that the only available descriptions come from old residents who remember having seen them. With or without fireplaces, the usual twin chimneys were brought out at the ridge even though precariously inclined between the loft floor and the ridge pole. Sometimes the angle was so acute that a split log was set alongside as a permanent brace to hold the brick chimney.

The Braemer house, while quite well disguised at the present time due to asbestos siding obscuring all of the half-timber work, possesses another unusual feature in the form of a brick vaulted cellar underneath the house. A series of segmental barrel-vaults is supported by masonry walls which, in turn, are pierced by segmental arched openings. The purpose of such elaborate subterranean masonry was to provide a cool cellar for the storage of perishables in the summertime and to afford a frost resistive winter storage place for preserves, potatoes and other root vegetables. Additionally, all food supplies in such a cellar were very effectively protected from loss by fire. Potatoes were stored in very large quantities because they were also fed to the hogs after being cooked in a large iron kettle. The German farmers of this period had not yet become accustomed to feeding hogs corn or maize which they called *tuerkischer Weizen*, meaning Turkish wheat.

Probably the oldest half-timber house of

German provenance in Wisconsin is the Hilgendorf house near Freistadt in Ozaukee County. Freistadt is the oldest German settlement in the state, having been founded by about twenty German Lutheran families who settled there in October of 1839. Most of them came from the Prussian province of Pomerania and spoke the low German, *Plattdeutsch*, dialect. At that time Ozaukee County was part of Washington County and Freistadt was located in Town IX thereof. The Hilgendorf house, now very adequately restored by the present owner and direct descendant of the original owner and builder, had fallen into serious disrepair after many years of use as a henhouse. As a fine specimen of half-timber work its timely rescue is to be applauded. This house discloses some interesting deviations from the usual pattern. The profile is relatively broad due to low ceiling heights and a fairly low-pitched roof. Absent also are the long diagonal corner braces and, instead, short length knee-braces were used. The nogging in the panels consists of rubble masonry composed of small chips of limestone taken from the ledge which crops out of the ground in this area of the county. A thin coat of lime plaster was applied to both sides of the panels. Interior partitions were similarly constructed. The date of this venerable house is 1845 or possibly earlier, and the builder was Ludwig Hilgendorf.

Curious because of its small size is the Zettler cottage which originally stood near Waukesha but now relocated in the Ozaukee County Pioneer Village. Consisting of but one room and a kitchen with a loft above, this tiny house was nevertheless built in the best half-timber fashion. Approximately 16 by 20 feet in size, the house had been relegated to a catch-all storage building and shop such as found on almost every older Wisconsin farmstead. Karl Zettler built this house in 1849. Its placement in an appropriate outdoor museum setting

HILGENDORF HOUSE near Freistadt. Restored structure seen from northeast.

ZETTLER HOUSE near Waubeka, now in Ozaukee County Pioneer Village, west elevation.

LUESKOW-MUELLER HOUSE near Iron Ridge, now in Old World Wisconsin, viewed from southwest.

KUENZI BARN near Watertown, seen from southeast.

CHRISTIAN BARN near Watertown, south elevation.

marks another entry on the credit side of the preservation ledger. Sharing attention with the Zettler Cottage in its new location is the Draeger house, originally situated near Woodland, and now a showpiece half-timber structure fully restored. The Draeger house was built in 1847.

Somewhat larger than the Zettler cottage but still diminutive in scale is the old Mueller house, built in 1850 in the Town of Herman, Dodge County. Now relocated in *Old World Wisconsin*, this small half-timber house has been converted to a ticket office while still retaining its original features. The name has also been changed to reflect that of the builder and original owner, so it is now the Lueskow house. This policy in nomenclature is sometimes at variance with the application of commonly used names by which old buildings have been generally known over the years and when the original owner's name lacks any kind of currency.

As to barns, among the best surviving half-timber specimens is the Kuenzi barn in the vicinity of Watertown. It is 46 by 20 feet in size and believed to have been built around 1850 by Ferdinand Paetsch. The timber is oak and the nogging is red Hustisford brick, with exceptionally good texture and interesting color variations. For many years it has been utilized as a pig barn. In close proximity is the Christian barn, also with an oak timber frame but with panel nogging of buff Watertown brick. This barn, 40 by 15 feet at the lower floor, has an overhanging second story along the south side. Ludwig Mielenz is thought to have built this barn about 1850 and it, too, has served as a pig barn for a long time. It has not been possible to determine whether this was the original use.

Half-timber work was used not only for houses and barns but also for commercial buildings and churches. Only one commercial building is known to have survived and it has sustained some major alterations, particularly on the inside. This structure was built in 1855 by Ernst Klessig, a brewmaster and innkeeper, and is located in Fillmore, Washington County. At one time is was known as the Saxonia House and came to be regarded as the hub of social events in this part of the county. The Klessig family lived in this building which also housed a small brewery. The beer was *lagered* in caves, so-called, which were located on the south end of the property. Negotiations are underway to acquire this structure for *Old World Wisconsin*, anticipating that it will be placed on the west side of the mall of the Visitor Center.

KLESSIG HOUSE AND BREWERY, Fillmore, view looking southeast.

As to churches, the only known survivor is the Lutheran Kripplein Christi Church near Iron Ridge in Dodge County which was built in 1864 by Pomeranian Prussian immigrants who had settled in the area a few years earlier. The interior has been renovated a number of times and the exterior walls have been covered with artificial stone of some sort, thereby totally obscuring the original half-timber work. But, at least, the church is still standing which is more than can be said of another Dodge County church, St. Paul's at Woodland, and the second church known to have been built at Freistadt in Ozaukee County by Trinity Evangelical Lutheran congregation in 1844. The Woodland church was built around 1860, probably under the aegis of the Reverend Wilhelm Schimpf. The parsonage was situated at the back end of the church building. The pulpit was in the center of the easterly wall of the nave and directly accessible from the parsonage. St. Paul's was a handsome half-timber structure, following quite closely its European prototypes. The nogging between the oak timbers was red Hustisford brick. For reasons not altogether clear, St. Paul's church was demolished in 1891, and a lone photograph is all that remains to indicate what it may have looked like. While no photographs of the Freistadt church have ever been found, a very detailed description is contained in the *Chronica*, a record book prepared and kept by the Reverend L. F. E. Krause, the first pastor at Freistadt from 1841 to 1847. Contemporary records suggest that the Reverend Krause was a redoubtable personality and never to be taken lightly, but the man unquestionably had a sense of history. His account of the building of the church, beginning with the felling of the trees and ending with the placing of the copper ball and sheet-iron weather cock on the steeple is so clear and detailed that when combined with known contemporary practice in *Fachwerk* construction the wall-framing pattern can be established with remarkable fidelity. On the basis of this record, construction drawings of the Freistadt church have been prepared by the writer, and it would, therefore, be possible to undertake a facsimile with confidence as to accuracy of form and detail.

Apparently the Freistadt half-timber church began to develop foundation difficulties shortly after it was built, leading to the conclusion that the timber sills were laid directly on the ground, possibly supported only at the corners and intermediate points with large flat boulders. Evidently, the pioneer builders, thinking themselves in the latitude of central Italy, were unaware of the severity of Wisconsin winters, the depth to which frost would penetrate and the degree to which resultant heaving of the earth would occur. In the case of the first log structures, frankly regarded as provisional by their builders, the urgency of their being erected quickly made the absence of elaborate foundations understandable. But, the Freistadt church — a *Fachwerk* structure — was clearly not a temporary building. Carefully selected oak timbers hewed and framed, mortised, tenoned and pegged in the best European tradition bespeaks a permanent structure. The use of kiln-burned brick nogging, pargetted inside and outside, further supports this impression. It was obviously the absence of adequate foundations that limited the use of the church to something like 22 years. This type of structural failure, while curious, was not actually uncommon and often led to premature disintegration of the entire structure. The record shows that Trinity church began having trouble as early as October, 1861, and discussions were initiated about building a new church. The majority, however, voted to save the half-timber church by underpinning it with a new foundation. This was done in the spring of 1863, but the remedy apparently was not entirely successful. In the summer of 1870 the church was dismantled and the brick sold at fifty cents per load.

While limited pretty much to Wisconsin in terms of quantity, German half-timber work — *Fachwerbau* — was one of the most significant regional architectural phenomena of the nineteenth century in America, yet its very existence went completely unheeded by architectural historians until first noted and recorded by the writer in 1953. Following a series of articles giving impetus to the idea of saving some of the state's best specimens of half-timber work, literally dozens of excellent examples were turned up, thereby demonstrating that this type of construction was not simply a curiosity of little architectural consequence but, instead, a major historic manifestation. It may be that earlier historiographers, including those of the Historic American Buildings Survey of the 1930s, simply did not know about half-timber work or, if they did, to ignore it as having no stylistic significance. The latter is a distinct possibility in view of the attitude prevalent even today that to have any validity, architecture and its history must be viewed through the eyes of the art historian in terms of style and surface cosmetics. Of course, this is a myopic apprehension. The ranks of the genuine *cognoscenti*, while never very ample in any discipline, certainly are not identifiable as belonging exclusively to the art history department.

TRINITY EVANGELICAL LUTHERAN CHURCH, Freistadt. Reconstruction drawing of northwest elevation based on Pastor Krause's Chronica.

ST. PAUL'S EVANGELICAL LUTHERAN CHURCH near Woodland. West elevation as seen on photograph dating from 1885. Photo courtesy of Mrs. Mathilda Wartchow.

ST. AUGUSTINE ROMAN CATHOLIC CHURCH, New Diggings, detail of cornice and corner pilaster.

Open Timber Framing

Following the early pioneer log structures and chronologically overlapping half-timber work, the open timber frame — also known as the full frame or braced frame — was used for virtually every type of building throughout the nineteenth century. Its popularity, particularly in Wisconsin, extended well into the present century until supplanted by lighter framing techniques. It was enhanced by what, at the time, must have seemed a limitless supply of raw material in the form of softwood coming in from Wisconsin's northern forests, and coupled with advances in the manufacture of iron and steel which led to the development of improved saws and woodworking tools including, most importantly, the invention of machine-cut nails. The open timber frame consisted of the same basic components as the half-timber frame, but as time went on hewn timbers gradually yielded to sawn material and there was less and less connecting of the timbers by notching, mortising and tenoning. Wood pegs were replaced by iron nails of all sizes and even the heaviest timbers were spiked together with 6 inch long 60d nails. Because the timbers were no longer exposed as had been the case in half-timber work, the framing pattern became less regular and the spacing of members was made to accommodate the architectural style of the building with particular reference to the placement of door and window openings. Lacking the rigidity of the masonry nogged half-timber frame, the open frame had to be stiffened by other means and usually by the application of board sheathing on the outside and sometimes on the inside also.

The nineteenth century was marked by the advent of several architectural revivals. The most notable ones were the Greek Revival and Gothic Revival. In Wisconsin, as elsewhere, wood frame buildings often formed the skeletons to which Classic Greek as well as Gothic details were applied, although the prototypes in either case had been stone buildings. Unlike the early log and half-timber buildings which were simple and unaffected, architecture became self-conscious, although certainly not always without charm and grace. The facility with which wood could now be made to imitate stone gave rise to decoration and ornament heretofore considered unattainable. To the credit of the early revivalist architects and builders, their work, while imitative, was generally done in simple, good taste — a quality which was lost in much of the Victorian work following the Civil War.

Thomas Jefferson is often credited with being the father of Greek Revival in America. Actually, however, Jefferson was mainly interested in the architecture of Rome and of the Roman Republic at that. While he was intensely concerned with everything classic, including architecture, there certainly was nothing Grecian in his work, and his Roman was so thoroughly modified as to constitute a unique Jeffersonian style. Thomas Jefferson obviously saw an analogy between the young Republic of the New World and the old Roman Republic. At any rate, his admiration for classic Roman architecture led him to consider it as a suitable expression for buildings in America. By the same token, he had nothing but contempt for Georgian architecture which he felt to be not only too Baroque but also too British to be of any further use in America.

It was an English architect of French lineage, educated in German universities, who introduced Greek Revival to America. It was Benjamin Henry Latrobe who first gave some direction to the architectural movement which was to dominate American building from 1800 to the Civil War. Latrobe in also generally regarded as the founder of the architectural profession in the United States. Having been professionally trained as an architect and having achieved success abroad, his work became extremely popular in America. Although Latrobe had thorough knowledge of the classics and possessed great archaeological competence, he was not merely a copyist of classic forms in his solution of current architectural problems. He handled the Greek style with intelligence and understanding, and in a manner that would be called "free" even today. Unfortunately, Latrobe's competence and good sense were not often matched in the work of his copyist contemporaries and followers who were, for the most part, builders rather than trained professional architects. These builders knew little of ancient structural systems, and probably cared less, but they were determined to copy Greek and Roman forms, employing American methods of construction to achieve the results they wanted. Greek Revival, as a style, began to proliferate around 1820, the year of Latrobe's death. Before that, buildings done in what is sometimes known as the Neo-Classic manner had the mark of Latrobe on them. They were not a fad at all, but a genuine effort to develop a new and suitable architecture for a new society. The Greek Revival coincided with the need for new building types. This came at a time when great American sympathy was aroused for everything Greek because of the war of independence being waged by the Greeks against the Turks in 1821-1828, which reminded the American people of their own struggle for independence just a few years earlier. Accordingly, Greek mannerisms were affected not only in architecture but in such unrelated things as style in women's coiffure and clothing and names of cities. In this process, directly and indirectly, Wisconsin got some excellent Greek buildings as well as an Attica, an Athens, a Troy and a Sparta.

Here in Wisconsin, before the Civil War, many buildings showing Greek Revival influence were the work of "Yankee" carpenters. Many of these builders carried with them handbooks of design which they used to good advantage. One of the most popular of these handbooks was *The Young Builders General Instructor* published by 1829 by Minard LaFever, a New York architect. By means such as these, Greek Revival was brought to the far reaches of a rapidly expanding nation and far beyond the ministrations of the professional architect. These handbooks contained carefully drawn illustrations of entrances, cornices, capitals, mantels and moldings in beautiful adaptations of Greek forms. Also included were house plans generally reminiscent of Greek temples. Some were shown with wings

KUEHNEMAN house, Racine, southwest elevation.

COLLINS HOUSE, town of Caledonia, viewed from southwest.

COTTON HOUSE, Green Bay. Seen from southwest in Heritage Hill State Park.

and porches, together with carefully studied elevations of remarkable inventiveness and good taste. One characteristic feature of the Greek Revival house was the heavily molded gable facing the street. Frequently there was a portico, and occasionally the columns were made square for reasons of economy. Often there was a low wing on one side, sometimes on both sides, with the ridge at right angles to the main ridge. The main entrance door was usually set between sidelights with a rectangular transom above. An elaborate entrance sometimes had fluted, engaged columns between the doors and the sidelights. Sidelights and transoms were often glazed with handsomely executed leaded glass panels. The whole was generally framed in heavily molded trim, or set between pilasters with a broad entablature. Many of these houses with their good proportions and refined detail have a charm and an air of quiet dignity about them which, somehow, got lost in some of the later Victorian work.

Just such a house, and one of the finest surviving examples of domestic Greek Revival architecture in Wisconsin, is the Kuehneman house on South Main Street in Racine. While its exact origin is not known, it is thought that the house may have been designed by the architect, Lucas Bradley, for Eli Cooley, mayor of Racine, in about 1853. Known for years as the Dyer house, because of its being the home of Federal Judge Dyer from 1871 to 1892, the house was later owned by the Taylor family and, more recently, by Mr. and Mrs. Kuehneman who are to be credited with its restoration. It is a so-called Temple house of the Greek Revival period, consisting of a two story center wing having a full height portico of four Doric columns on the front. The center portion is symmetrically flanked by two one and one-half story wings. The moldings and other details give evidence of excellent taste and great refinement. The interiors, replete with marble fireplace mantels and a handsome staircase are among the best of their kind in Wisconsin. The Kuehneman house is a fairly late expression of Greek Revival as the style had passed its crest elsewhere in the country and Victorianisms of all sorts were already in vogue, especially in the east.

A few miles northwest of Racine on the Nicholson Road in the Town of Caledonia, in Racine County, is another Temple house which might be called a country cousin of the Kuehneman house. The central Doric tetraprostyle resembles the Kuehneman house so very much that it could be assumed that either the same architect or the same architectural handbook played a part in its design. The house is believed to have been built around 1853 by an early settler named Collins who had come to the area from New York state. Unlike the Kuehneman house, the Collins house has only one flanking wing to the south which, so it was said, had been added in the 1870s. However, while undertaking some major alterations, the present owner discovered that the wing, presumed to have been a wing, was really the original house probably dating from the early 1840s, to which the Temple house had been added. The Collins house never received the sympathetic care enjoyed by the Kuehneman house but the present owner is undertaking some restorative treatment which may still serve to prolong its longevity.

Also in the Temple style, but on a somewhat grander scale is the Cotton house in Green Bay. Now situated on South Webster Avenue, the house was moved to this location from its original site and is now embodied in Green Bay's Heritage Hill State Park. Built of wood, the portico consists of a two story arrangement of two Doric columns set into a recess which is known as distyle-in-antis. The house was built by Captain Winslow Cotton in 1835. This

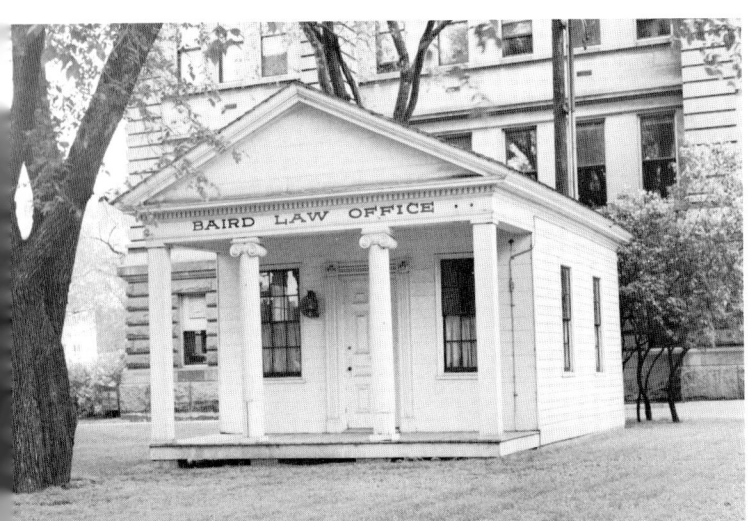

BAIRD LAW OFFICE, Green Bay. Seen from east while temporarily located on grounds of Brown County courthouse.

WHITE PILLARS, De Pere, viewed from southeast.

YORK house, near Zenda, south elevation.

house is an excellent example of first-rate restoration, and its tastefully appointed interiors are open to the public.

Two additional Temple buildings, but of rather diminutive scale, may be found in the Green Bay area. The first is the Baird Law Office, now relocated directly north of the Cotton house in the state park. It is an Ionic tetraprostyle porticoed one story building and was built in 1831 for Henry Baird, the first lawyer to establish a practice west of the Great Lakes, and Wisconsin's first Attorney General. Happily, this little building also has been preserved and restored for posterity. The other little building is a private residence known as White Pillars, and is located on North Broadway in De Pere. A Doric tetraprostyle porticoed one story house, its original function was that of a bank. It was built in 1836 for the Fox River Bank which later became Kellogg's Bank. Of unusually small scale, its outstanding feature is the high relief ornament in the tympanum of the pediment. Considering the time and place of construction, this embellishment is uncommon. While in private ownership and already altered extensively on the inside, the house does not appear to be endangered, but it is such an unusual specimen of Greek Revival that it deserves close attention with an eye to eventual preservation and restoration.

Another typical Greek Revival expression, but quite different from the Temple variety, is the pilastered, two story, side-entrance type of house which came into rather common use during the 1840s and 1850s. Not many good examples have survived unaltered and unscathed, but a rather typical specimen remains near Zenda in Walworth County, almost on the Illinois state line. This is the York house, built about 1845. It is in need of attention and merits preservation.

In the same vein, though somewhat more formal, is the Sanford-Duerst house, near Whitewater in Walworth County. Believed to have been built about 1850, it is a symmetrically disposed house with two flanking wings, all wood clapboarded with an open timber structural frame. Vacant for many years, the house has, by the same token, remained relatively unaltered. Negotiations are under way at the present time to acquire this building for *Old World Wisconsin*.

Other variations on the Greek Revival theme produced distinctly atypical houses such as the Cooper house on State Highway 20 just west of Waterford. Built by James Cooper of New York state about 1840, this open wood frame, clapboarded house is clearly identifiable as Greek Revival, even though it has little in common with the Temple house or the typical side-entrance house. It is a one and one-half story building with a longitudinal recessed porch and a one story flanking wing similarly treated with a recessed porch. Small windows under the frieze give this house a very distinctive appearance.

SANFORD-DUERST HOUSE, Whitewater vicinity, southeast elevation.

COOPER *house, near Waterford, southwest elevation.*

ELA HOUSE, *Rochester, east elevation.*

Just east of the bridge and on the bank of the Fox River in Rochester stands the Ela house, built in 1838 by Richard Emerson Ela, carriage and wagon maker of Lebanon, New Hampshire. Also of wood frame, this house is yet another variation of Greek Revival, almost New England Colonial in feeling, with its two story central mass, unsymmetrical elevations and one story wing at the southwest corner. A denticulated cornice and main entrance pediment are particularly interesting features of this house.

Demonstrating that Greek Revival architecture was never a stereotype is the Balfanz house on Sixth Street in Prairie du Sac. Built by Edward Perkins in 1842, this two story wood building, with a one and one-half story wing at the south end, has the unusual treatment of a continuous one story porch with seven square wood columns extending across the front. Highly refined details at the entrances and cornice mark this building as being derived from the hand of a skilled and original designer.

ALFANZ house, Prairie du Sac, southeast elevation.

WADE HOUSE, Greenbush, southeast elevation.

GRIGNON house, Kaukauna, south elevation.

In Kaukauna, the Grignon house, now beautifully restored, is still another variation of the Greek Revival theme. This house, an open frame clapboarded structure, was built in 1836 by Charles Augustin Grignon. Again, it is a two story main building with a one story kitchen wing, but its unique feature is the five bay, balustraded, square colonnaded porch, with a two story portico over the main entrance. The building was in ruinous condition at one time, but has been successfully restored and is now open to visitors.

During the middle years of the nineteenth century, many stagecoach inns were built along the plank roads that connected the principal communities in Wisconsin. Only a few of these important landmarks have survived. Among them are the Wade House at Greenbush, Hawks Inn at Delafield, and the Dunkel Inn in Brookfield. All are open timber frame, wood clapboarded structures, carried out in Greek Revival style. The Wade House, now the property of the State Historical Society of Wisconsin, was retrieved from

HAWKS INN, Delafield, north elevation.

DOUSMAN-DUNKEL-BEHLING HOUSE, Brookfield, southeast elevation.

oblivion and restored through the generosity of the Kohler Foundation. Hawks Inn, also scheduled for destruction, has been relocated and fully restored by local preservationists. The Dunkel Inn, now more fully named Dousman-Dunkel-Behling Inn, is an exceptionally handsome building and when measured up during the Historic American Buildings Survey of 1934 was found to have been framed of black walnut timber, from which it may be assumed that the Brookfield area abounded with groves of this now precious cabinet wood that it could be used for such utilitarian purposes. The ultimate fate of the Dousman-Dunkel-Behling Inn hangs in the balance because of the proposed widening of Blue Mound Road. Fortunately, a dedicated local preservation group is actively engaged in developing a program to move the building to park land several hundred yards north on Moorland Road, and thereafter to undertake its complete and proper restoration.

The Greek Revival style also made a distinct impression on open timber framed wood churches built in Wisconsin between 1840 and 1860. Again, while very numerous at one time, only a few good specimens of church architecture in Greek Revival style have come down to the present time. Their care and maintenance becomes a serious responsibility if the preservation of these valuable buildings is to be assured. Variations similar to those found in domestic work of the period are also found in contemporary church architecture. Some religious groups which stressed simplicity and modesty in all things, built Greek Revival church buildings of the meeting house type. One of these is the Scotch Meetinghouse in the Town of Dover, Racine County, standing only one story high, and of extremely simple lines and chaste details. It has not been used for many years and its future is uncertain.

Another meetinghouse of simplest Greek

Revival lines is the Painesville Chapel on the Ryan Road at Highway 41, in Franklin. This building was erected in 1832 by Henry Roethe as the meetinghouse of a German Freethinkers' society. Judging from the sentiments of some of the old gravestone inscriptions and other documentation, this society seems to have subscribed to Jeffersonian deism and, therefore, hardly militantly atheistic.

A somewhat larger meetinghouse may be found in the Town of Vernon, Waukesha County. Vacant since 1920, this church was built in 1854 by a reformed Presbyterian group known as Scotch Covenanters, and appears to be the only church ever to be built by this denomination in Wisconsin. Rigidly Calvinistic in doctrine, the theological discipline of the Covenanters is reflected in its church architecture, for which simple Greek Revival was eminently suited. This structure, together with its adjoining cemetery should be seriously regarded as a preservation prospect. The churchyard alone, with its gravestones, tells a poignant story of what Wisconsin pioneer life was like with entire families wiped out by diptheria, smallpox, cholera and other epidemial disasters, to say nothing of the hazards of child-bearing and simply, the dangers of everyday living.

SCOTCH MEETINGHOUSE, town of Dover, seen from southeast.

PAINESVILLE CHAPEL, Franklin, south elevation.

SCOTCH COVENANTER MEETING HOUSE, town of Vernon, viewed from southwest.

SEVENTH DAY BAPTIST church at Albion, southwest elevation.

Greek Revival church towers, of which there are few, fall into three general categories; the open belfry, the square enclosed belfry, and the octagon and spire. A good example of the open belfry type is that of the Seventh Day Baptist Church at Albion in Dane County, erected in 1843. Situated among fine old trees, this church faces the Seventh Day Baptist College campus, and has been kept in good repair.

A typical enclosed square belfry is that of the Muskego Meetinghouse at Prospect, built in 1859 as a Free-Will Baptist Church. Used for worship and related purposes until 1925, the building is now a community hall. In addition to its tower, the outstanding feature of this edifice is the sunburst treatment of the tympanum in the front gable.

The First Baptist Church at Merton in Waukesha County, built in 1845 by a congregation composed predominantly of families from New England, exemplifies the smaller wood frame church with octagon and spire. Few churches of this type seem to have been built, as the tendency was more in the direction of square and relatively small belfries.

MUSKEGO MEETING HOUSE, Prospect, viewed from southeast.

FIRST BAPTIST church at Merton, northwest elevation.

During the years in which Greek Revival enjoyed its greatest popularity, Gothic Revival influences also began to be felt. This was particularly true in church design, with the result that some rather curious mixtures of Greek and Gothic motives were developed. Generally, these mixtures were most common in wood frame church buildings. The Moravian church at Green Bay, built in 1851, has typical Greek Revival lines and details except for the windows and the tower. These are Gothic Revival, resulting in a curious but not unpleasant blend.

A similar combination of Greek and Gothic details appears on the Methodist church at Green Lake. Here, except for the tower which is Greek Revival, the building has Gothic lines, including windows and the scroll-sawed verge boards. The church was built around 1850.

METHODIST *church at Green Lake, detail of tower and vergeboards.*

MORAVIAN *church at Green Bay, north elevation.*

METHODIST *church at Green Lake, northwest elevation.*

ST. PETER ROMAN CATHOLIC CHURCH Milwaukee and St. Francis, now Old World Wisconsin, viewed from southeast.

Old St. Peter's church, built in 1839 at Jackson and State Streets in Milwaukee, and believed to be the oldest Roman Catholic church edifice in Wisconsin, is another example of the fusion of Gothic and Greek Revival elements. After several moves around the Milwaukee area, old St. Peter's was finally brought to *Old World Wisconsin* and thoughtfully restored to its 1889 appearance, thereby making it appear the way it seems to have looked fifty years after it was built. The Knights of Columbus played a very active role in the preservation of this very significant building.

Perhaps the most unusual of the Greek and Gothic Revival combinations is St. Augustine church at New Diggings in Lafayette County. Built in 1844 by Father Samuel Mazzuchelli, priest and architect, this building displays an Italianate variation of Greek Revival combined with Gothic Revival elements. It has an open bell tower, pointed arch openings and a Greek fret cornice. The wood board siding was cut to simulate rusticated stonework. Louvered shutters over wood muntined windows soften and filter the natural light that enters the nave. Standing vacant for many years St. Augustine had reached a level of serious deterioration when the Knights of Columbus, aided by a generous anonymous donor again came to the rescue. The church has been saved but continuing care and maintenance are necessary to prevent future deterioration. This outstanding old building is such an important element of Wisconsin's cultural legacy that its preservation should be regarded as a public responsibility even though it is not public property.

The Gothic Revival began in England and the Continent during the eighteenth century, starting as an offshoot of the Romantic movement in literature and music, and was

ST. AUGUSTINE ROMAN CATHOLIC CHURCH, New Diggings, south elevation.

ST. AUGUSTINE ROMAN CATHOLIC CHURCH, New Diggings, detail of belfry.

first regarded as a rich man's hobby. It turned out to be more than a passing fad and, instead, became an important symbol of ascendant nationalism. In England it continued to grow, fostered by writers such as Sir Walter Scott whose delineations of England's glorious mediaeval past were enchanting to people who were becoming weary of the sometimes pompous formalities of an imported classic culture. So, side by side, grew Gothic and Greek Revival with Gothic, in the end, achieving somewhat greater longevity.

In Germany and France, the Gothic Revival had much the same causes behind it as in England. A wave of restoration activities swept the Continent and many mediaeval buildings were rebuilt and sometimes completed after a time lag of centuries. In the case of Cologne cathedral, for example, drawings of the west front — as proposed but never carried out — were discovered early in the nineteenth century, and forthwith the construction of the now famous twin-spired west front was undertaken. Not the least of considerations prompting this venture was national pride in German achievement.

Naturally, a movement as widespread as the Gothic Revival in Europe was bound to be felt in the United States. Its first indications here, very early in the nineteenth century, suggested novelty and innovation, but little else. Gradually, however, the style gained popular acceptance and soon became a dominant element in American architectural design. It was not true Gothic, of course, and architects generally did not even attempt to embody Gothic structural principles in their buildings. They were satisfied to obtain merely its appearance, often by the use of sham materials.

HOLY INNOCENTS *church at Nashotah, south elevation, now demolished.*

ST. JOHN CHRYSOSTOM *church at Delafield, northeast elevation.*

Although Gothic Revival flourished on the Atlantic seaboard in particular, examples were found in the Midwest up to the Mississippi River Valley, including Wisconsin. Popular handbooks for builders and the writings of such enthusiasts as Andrew Jackson Downing gave impetus to Gothic Revival of one sort or another, not only in larger cities and towns, but in rural locations as well. Local materials were extensively employed, and since masonry was not considered necessary, the style had frequent expressions in wood. Some of this work was sometimes referred to as "Carpenter Gothic." While anything but true Gothic, many of these buildings had a peculiar charm, particularly those with a straightforward timber frame, a steep roof and scroll-sawed gable ends, together with high, narrow windows set in board walls with batten strips over the joints.

For many years Wisconsin was fortunate in still having several churches of this type, but very recently one of them was lost. This was Holy Innocents Church at Nashotah. Built in 1861, it had a heavy oak frame with heavy boards and battens, and an open bell-cote at the west end. Buildings such as this are irreplaceable.

Of the same chapel type, and fortunately still standing, is St. John Chrysostom Church at Delafield. It is said that the plans for this church followed those of a parish church at Greenstead in England. More recent inquiry indicates very strongly that the architect was Richard Upjohn, of New York, whose work includes Trinity Church on Wall Street and Broadway in that city. Plans, elevations and details almost identical with those of St. John Chrysostom appear in *Upjohn's Rural Architecture*, published in 1852. Actually, St. John Chrysostom Church was built one year earlier — 1851 — but it may be assumed that Upjohn provided the design in any case. The building is also a heavy oak timber frame covered with wide vertical boards and battens. No plaster was used and other ideas and materials were in accord with a liturgical trend in the Anglican Church known as the Oxford Movement. Pierced tracery verge boards distinguish the exterior and the appearance of the whole is enhanced by its hilltop location and the adjoining free-standing wood bell tower. The plank doors of the church are hung on beautifully wrought iron hinges, which were made by Jacob Luther, the village blacksmith, who also provided all of the hand-forged nails used throughout the building. Alden S. Kelly was the carpenter who built the church.

No discussion of Wisconsin frame buildings would be complete without including some of the early farm buildings which were not only handsome in appearance but exceptionally well-made. Most unfortunately, they are disappearing from the landscape at an alarming rate. With the increasing mechanization of all agricultural activities, many old barns are functionally obsolete. Unwilling to maintain buildings that have outlived their usefulness, most owners simply neglect them until they are beyond repair. As a result, even some of the more interesting specimens such as the steep-roofed Norwegian barns once found in the Edgerton and Stoughton area of Dane County are all but extinct. The Swiss and Pennsylvania type barns of Green County have fared somewhat better, but it is no longer possible to find a completely unaltered specimen. The resemblance of some of these barns to Pennsylvania work is not coincidence. Green County is generally identified with Swiss immigrants from Canton Glarus because of the Swiss cheese industry, but the earliest settlers were Pennsylvania Germans who brought with them a pioneering experience extending over several generations on American soil. While their first barns were, as usual, modest log structures, increasing prosperity permitted the

NORWEGIAN BARN near Stoughton. Southwest elevation of pioneer structure, now demolished.

RUPNOW BARN near New Glarus. Pennsylvania-Swiss type, southeast elevation.

FREITAG BARN near Monticello. Pennsylvania-Swiss type, viewed from southeast.

CLAUSING BARN, Mequon, now in Old World Wisconsin, south elevation.

OCTAGONAL barn near Hollandale, southeast elevation.

building of barns in the best Pennsylvania tradition. Set upon a fieldstone foundation, pierced by numerous "Dutch" doors, the spacious superstructures often had an overhang known as a *Vorschuss,* and several round-headed, vertical, louvered ventilators in the wood frame walls. To see what remains of the once numerous assortment of Swiss-Pennsylvania barns, a leisurely ride along the town roads of Green and Rock Counties may prove very rewarding.

A wood frame barn almost unique to Wisconsin is the octagonal type, and at one time quite numerous in what is now the City of Mequon, Ozaukee County. The ranks of these barns are also being decimated rapidly because of their being located in the path of expanding urbanization. Legend has it that these barns were built in octangular form to better resist the strong winds coming off Lake Michigan, but it is difficult to dismiss the influence of the north German *Rundscheunen* or the work and writings of Orson Fowler which enjoyed considerable popularity during the second half of the nineteenth century. Most of the Mequon area barns were built by a German carpenter named Ernst Clausing, and at one time there were fourteen of these barns along the Port Washington Road between Milwaukee and Port Washington — a distance of about twenty-five miles. The unusual feature of these barns is the amount of open space they provide without interior posts or bearing walls. Generally set upon a fieldstone foundation, the wood frame superstructure at the hay-floor level is one large unobstructed area. The roof rafters are joined together near the top by an octagonal timber collar. Similarly, the plates upon which the rafters rest are tied together with angle irons to make a continuous ring of the plate, thus converting the lateral thrusts of the roof into vertical loads upon the outside bearing walls. The roofs of the octagonal barns were generally crowned with louvered or glazed cupolas. One of the best of the Clausing barns was donated to *Old World Wisconsin* and fully restored. It now houses an exhibit hall on the first floor and a restaurant on the lower level.

Scattered wood frame octagonal barns may be found elsewhere in the state, but they are rare. A good specimen, but of different proportions than the Clausing barns, is a relatively small building near Hollandale in Iowa County. This barn has a buff limestone ashlar foundation with a timber frame superstructure and a terneplate roof. Besides being a very practical building, it has excellent proportions and makes an interesting picture with the adjoining round, red brick silo.

Several round, open frame barns in the state are also worth notice. One is the Christianson barn near Deerfield in Dane County, and the other one, the Schreiber barn, is located in New Berlin, Waukesha County. In these barns the silo is set in the center and the roof construction radiates about it. The foundations are built of fieldstone masonry in both instances.

Polygonal barns are also to be found and among the best of these are the Whitney barn near Pittsville in Wood County and the Lueder-Laack barn near Plymouth, Sheboygan County. Both are wood timber frame structures of about the same diameter but there are some significant differences. The Whitney barn is twelve-sided and is set directly on the ground without any foundation or basement treatment. The first floor level is only slightly above the adjoining grade, and is used for the stabling of cattle. The second floor opens up into a spacious haw mow. In the center is a large double-walled brick silo. The roof is framed of continuous rafters to form the double gambrel, which resembles the inverted hull of a ship. Four-hipped roof dormers admit light to the upper level. Each leg of the duodecagonal plan

CHRISTIANSON round barn near Deerfield, east elevation.

CHRISTIANSON round barn near Deerfield. Interior view showing silo and roof framing.

SCHREIBER BARN, New Berlin, west elevation.

WHITNEY BARN near Pittsville, west elevation.

LUEDER-LAACK BARN near Plymouth, south elevation.

is eighteen feet in length, giving the barn an approximate diameter of sixty feet. The Whitney barn was built in 1912 and has received excellent maintenance.

The Lueder-Laack barn has a thirteen-sided plan. Also open timber framed, it rests upon a masonry foundation consisting of both fieldstone and brickwork. It has a center silo of cast concrete and the hay-floor has a mezzanine to maximize space. The roof is also a gambrel, but of an easier slope than the Whitney with which it does share a few other attributes such as four hip-roofed dormers to admit light to the upper reaches of the interior. A thirteen-sided wood louvered cupola corresponding to the silo in diameter caps the entire composition. This barn was built in 1916 by Rudolph Lueder and is now in the ownership of his grandson, Howard Laack.

Although the octagonal, polygonal and round wood frame barns are not generally of the earliest pioneer period, having been built toward the end of the nineteenth and beginning of the present century, their kind is no longer being built. Their rapid disappearance must therefore be a matter of genuine concern from the standpoint of historic buildings preservation, since they are pioneer landmarks in every sense of the word.

The Balloon Frame

Somewhere around the mid-1830s, a new method of wooden house building emerged in the Chicago area, which was to make houses of wood cheaper and more popular then they already were, and change the apperance of every community in the land as well as the countryside itself. This was the balloon frame. While its exact origins are not altogether clear, to say nothing of its etymology, the time and place are fairly definite. There is also a belief, which has gained considerable currency, that the invention of the balloon frame was completely spontaneous and instantaneous — a sort of "big bang" hypothesis. As it happens, there are enough transitional framing specimens still in existence to demonstrate that, chronologically, the braced timber frame and the balloon frame overlapped for several decades, and, in some buildings, elements of each are to be found. As a matter of fact, there was an intervening development in wood framing known as the platform frame which retained much of the old braced frame but made use of slimmer, more closely spaced vertical members. Instead of running any vertical studs or posts up two stories, they were limited to one story in height and topped with a plate and the blind-floor of the second story, thus forming a platform upon which the construction of the second story proceeded similarly. In platform framing, the studs were rarely over three inches thick and usually spaced twenty-four inches on center, although some cases have been found in which sixteen inch spacing was used and which is standard practice even today. In balloon framing all studs for outside walls extended full two stories in height and the floor joists were supported on ribbands — one by six strips let into the studs. The objective was speed, strength, economy and efficient construction in which everything could be held together with nails. No more notching, mortising, tenoning or wood pegging became the order of the day. Two inches became the standard thickness for studs, rafters and joists alike — although in practice this dimension became gradually diminished, so that today it barely scales one and one-half inches. It will be borne in mind that balloon framing in all its aspects was and is a method to build houses and not much by way of other wooden structures. It met a specific need as the demand for houses grew in fast growing cities and new industrial centers during the nineteenth century. Facilitating the new technique was the growing availability of sawn lumber comparatively reasonable in price, and an expanding railway system making delivery possible almost everywhere in the country.

The platform frame and the balloon frame, while innovative and ultimately revolutionary in their effect upon timber building practice, at first did not usually extend beyond the limits of the larger urban areas. The speed with which balloon frame construction could meet the needs of a city such as Milwaukee was of small moment to the Wisconsin farmer and rural builder who had plenty of time, but who often lacked the cash to buy mill-made lumber and woodwork. Accordingly, the felling of trees, hewing and curing of timber, and joining them into a heavy frame, remained standard practice for most rural buildings until about 1870. Wisconsin barns were built this way well into the twentieth century. Eventually, of course, the heavy timber frame yielded completely to lighter forms of construction.

Part 2 Buildings of Brick

Solid Brick Walls

Brick is the world's oldest manufactured building material and, excepting pottery, probably the most important product ever to be made out of clay. From a sun-dried Chaldean tablet of nearly six-thousand years ago, we have evidence that man formed the clay of his river valleys into cakes, dried them in the sun, and used them for the walls of his buildings. Somewhat later, and probably discovered by accident, brick was burned by fire rather than merely dried in the sun. After the organization of the brick-mason's craft, which also seems to have occurred thousands of years before the Christian era, the masons themselves often manufactured the brick they used, thus contributing to the art of brickmaking as well as brickbuilding — a practice which continued well into modern times.

Naturally, our own beginnings in America, as well as here in Wisconsin, employed the art of brickmaking and brickbuilding as it was then practiced in Europe. Air-dried brick, consisting of mud, sand, pea-gravel and chopped straw, was occasionally used in connection with German half-timber work in southeastern Wisconsin during the early and middle part of the nineteenth century. Later on burned brick instead of air dried brick was used for nogging the panels and, of course, entire buildings were built of brick without the use of the timber frame. Such brick walls were usually solid and at least eight inches thick.

There are few places in Wisconsin where clay of one kind or another cannot be found. Even along river beds in such unlikely areas as the sand country of Adams, Juneau and Jackson Counties, clay may be found in substantial quantity. The clays are not uniform in composition and texture over any considerable area of the state but differ locally, depending on the source of the materials of which they may be composed. Nature had through centuries of time produced clay and shale deposits which differ from each other not so much in chemical composition as in physical structure, and most Wisconsin brick

Typical old Milwaukee building of the 1840 period, showing characteristics of the Federal style, stood on the corner of Milwaukee and Wells Streets. At one time there were hundreds of buildings like this. The last of them, including the one pictured, was torn down in the 1920s.

made during the early days was a clay rather than a shale product. Clay is nothing more than mud to most people, but clay suitable for brickmaking is technically known as hydrated silicate of alumina in which may occur substances such as oxides of iron, calcium, magnesium, potassium, sodium and sulphur. Clay is the disintegrated remains of rocks, themselves the product of the earliest periods of the formation of the earth and therefore basically igneous even though subsequently sedimentary in nature. During the geological periods that have intervened, a part of this clay has lain at its original site, and other parts have been torn away by glacial movements and successive winds, rains and floods, to be deposited at various levels and distances as sediment on the beds of rivers and lakes.

Pioneer brickmaking in Wisconsin was a small scale and largely do-it-yourself operation like most everything else that had to be done in connection with putting up a building. An interesting first-hand account of early day brickmaking is offered in Pastor L. F.E. Krause's *Chronica*, relating to the building of the half-timber church in Freistadt, at that time Washington County. In September, 1844, he made an entry that

> "the congregation awarded a contract . . . for making 40,000 finished and well burned brick at a price of $3.00 per thousand. Suitable clay was found near the schoolhouse, and on the 14th of August the molding of the brick began; and they turned out good. May God prosper the firing, that we may continue with the building of His house. They were molding brick until the 14th of September, and by the 20th the kilns had been set up and the firing began the same day. The firing ended the 28th of September. However, the bricks turned out too lean because the brick molders, to make things easier for themselves, had mixed in too much sand . . . Therefore, the brick molders were paid only $2.75 per thousand brick, to which they readily agreed."

Wisconsin clay made good brick, and for many years quite a variety was manufactured by literally scores of kilns throughout all parts of the state. The lacustrine or lake clays along Lake Michigan resulted in predominantly light cream and buff colored brick when properly made, while clays found elsewhere in the state produced various shades of red and brown brick. Outstanding among the early brick was that of Hustisford in Dodge County and Mineral Point in Iowa County because of good quality and exceptionally pleasant color in a blend of vermilion and burnt orange. A similar brick, but of somewhat more uniform red color, was produced in the Duck Creek area near Green Bay, in Forestville, Door County, and Menomonie in Dunn County. All along the Mississippi River and its tributaries on the west end of the state, various types of red, brown and russet colored bricks were made.

The cream colored brick produced in Milwaukee and vicinity earned for its home town the name "Cream City" and the brick itself became universally known as Cream City brick. While justly famous for its color, the first reactions were those of disappointment especially on the part of the Yankees to whom a brick was not a brick unless it had a fine ruddy color. Coupled with this there was additional disenchantment as the brick absorbed soot, dirt and grime which quickly grayed the bright yellow color. Nevertheless, Cream City brick was widely accepted and used in and around Milwaukee to the exclusion of nearly all other materials for more than fifty years. In Milwaukee with its half dozen brick yards, and elsewhere in the state, the manufacture of brick soon became more highly mechanized to meet the demand for a large supply for brick of even color and quality. This called for large scale operations and an almost inexhaustible source of uniform and reliable raw material such as found in Ohio and in the clay and shale pits of central Illinois near the coal beds which were just being opened. Then, because of improved transportation methods, especially by rail, Wisconsin's brick industry, almost always on a relatively small and localized basis, began to yield to mass-produced Illinois and Ohio imports. During Wisconsin's pioneer period, however, locally made brick played an important part in the development of Wisconsin architecture and the art of brickmaking.

Next to wood, brick offered the greatest versatility with which to meet the demands of current taste in design. Despite the nineteenth century tendency to excesses, there is discernible, nevertheless, a fine thread of good taste and discrimination which seems to have run through the otherwise coarse fabric of Victorian architecture. Buildings of brick were often simply designed and well-proportioned despite the trend toward the ornate and the unusual. Brick adaptions of Greek Revival and Gothic Revival designs, as well as completely astylar essays, occasionally resulted in buildings of considerable originality and charm. A small number of these structures has survived to the present time. Architectural carryovers from Colonial days and the Federal period that followed are also evident in a few early Wisconsin brick buildings that are still standing. Profile molded brick in belt courses and copings, while extremely rare in Wisconsin can, nevertheless, still be found in a few places. Brick cornices with unique denticulated effects are considerably more common, but time is taking its toll and not very many really good examples remain.

Many of Wisconsin's early nineteenth century buildings, and right up to the beginning of the Civil War period, were variations of the so-called Federal style. Generically related to the Post-Colonial and Greek Revival, the Federal style was characterized by lack of ornament and extreme simplicity, amounting almost to severity. The Federal style relied upon mass, scale and proportion, and frequently resulted in very distinguished architecture. Old lithographs showing panoramic views of Wisconsin cities during the mid-nineteenth century disclose a predominance of buildings in the Federal style, often carried out in brick as the principal material which lent itself admirably to the crisp lines demanded by the style.

As was the case with every American architectural period, the Federal style also had European counterparts. Principally, these were the Directoire and Empire styles in France, the Regency in England, and the so-called *Zopfstil* in Germany. As might be expected, these European contemporaries, especially the German, also exerted a discernible influence on Wisconsin architecture of that time. Following the usual sequence of architectural stylism, the Federal style and its European counterparts with their extremely simple lines represented a reaction to the

EATON HOUSE, Mineral Point, viewed from southeast.

WADE HOUSE, Mineral Point, southeast elevation.

POLSTER house near Mayville, southeast elevation.

opulence of eighteenth century rococo. Attempting to analyze the reasons for these changing trends, it becomes necessary to look at the socio-economic background of the times. It may also be that after a given length of time changes are made simply for the sake of change. It was Will Durant who said that "even perfection palls when it is long continued. Change is necessary to life, sensation and thought; an exciting novelty may seem by its very novelty to be beautiful, until the forgotten old returns on the wheel of time and is embraced as young and new."

The Federal style with its overtones of Neoclassicism was extremely popular in its day, but despite a popularity resulting in its becoming the dominant architectural expression for virtually every type of building during the first half of the nineteenth century, very few good examples have survived. Milwaukee, for example, had literally hundreds of these buildings in what now is the downtown and near downtown area still to be seen during the early years of the present century. Many were razed during the building boom of the 1920s and the rest were taken down in the 1950s and 1960s, so that today, for all practical purposes, this once important style of architecture is extinct as far as Milwaukee is concerned. It is only in the state's smaller communities that isolated examples are still to be found, and Mineral Point is one of them. Two particularly good houses with their characteristic chimneys at the gable ends are the Judge Parley Eaton house and the Wade house, both in Mineral Point. Both houses are built of local vermilion brick of exceptionally good color with cut, buff limestone lintels and trim. The Eaton house was erected in 1843 and has recently been very beautifully restored. The Wade house, also known as the Benson house or Hutchison house, has also been completely restored to its original condition and appearance by Dr. Correll. For many years this house had a two-story verandah and the entire building was painted white which gave it a very distinguished and almost southern apperance. This quality was lost in the restoration but the results are very creditable in showing what the house looked like when it was first built. Of the same mid-century vintage are the Polster house near Mayville and the Parlow house in Waubeka. Both are variations on the Federal theme with the latter, which was built for the Cooley family in 1851, having a captain's walk atop the roof of the main portion. The Meinhardt Bank at Burlington built in the 1840s is the Wisconsin's finest remaining example of a brick commercial structure in the Federal style. Now rehabilitated and remodeled, the Meinhardt Bank demonstrates the feasibility of restoring historic structures for a continuing useful purpose.

MEINHARDT BANK at Burlington, present appearance following recent alterations, northeast elevation.

PARLOW house at Waubeka, south elevation.

WHITAKER-LURVEY HOUSE near Dousman, southeast elevation.

DUNCAN house at Cooksville, east elevation.

A very popular house type of modified Federal style was the so-called "square" house, usually having a hipped roof, balanced elevations and the main entrance off to one side. Even of this once common type very few are left anywhere. One of them is the Lurvey house near Dousman which was built in 1856 by Col. Charles Whitaker. The brick is again a red-vermilion blend, and the lines of this house suggest the Italianate influence which was beginning to be felt during these pre-Civil War years. The house is in excellent condition and carefully maintained. A similar square house with some of the same design characteristics, though less Italianate, is the Duncan house in Cooksville, Rock County. Cooksville might be called a community of pioneer brick houses and happens to be one of Wisconsin's most charming settlements and, in a way, a ghost town in that its potential was never realized because the railway bypassed the place in 1857. First settled in 1840, most of the first residents came from New York state as second generation American pioneers whose fathers and grandfathers had left New England for the new territory opened up in northern New York early in the nineteenth century. The houses in Cooksville were built of locally made brick in a warm russet vermilion blend. The houses were built around a square block set aside in the center of the community as a village green, or common, and reserved for the use of all the families in traditional New England manner. In addition to the Duncan house, but leaning stylistically toward Gothic Revival are the Isaac Porter, the Hoxie and the Backenstoe-Howard houses — all treated with good domestic feeling, individuality and simplicity not always evident in this period. Cooksville is an unspoiled community — architecturally and historically significant — which deserves to be restored and preserved in perpetuity.

ISAAC PORTER *house at Cooksville, southeast elevation.*

HOXIE *house at Cooksville, southeast elevation.*

Comprising another variation of Wisconsin brickbuilding especially unique and original in character are the buildings of no specific derivative historical style in terms of classification, but which nevertheless constitute a definite, identifiable group. These are the buildings in which brick was used not only to build the walls, but also to supply the ornamental details such as cornices, belt courses and other decorative elements.

One of the finest of these, now destroyed, was the old Lehmann house at Richfield, built in 1853 by the first station master in that town. It was a tiny house of four rooms and of very diminutive scale in which the decorative use of brick for cornice and belt course could be seen at its best. The brick was of a pink and buff blend and of local origin. Affectionately known as the Old Shoemaker's House because of its last and long-time occupant, the house had been standing vacant for a number of years. Repeated incidents of vandalism followed, and all efforts to save the house ended in

BACKENSTOE-HOWARD *house at Cooksville, also known as "Waucoma Lodge," east elevation.*

LEHMANN HOUSE, Richfield. Viewed from southwest prior to demolition.

STEINKE HOUSE, Port Washington, now in Ozaukee County Pioneer Village, southwest elevation.

failure, but not before complete measured drawings were prepared by the writer prior to its demolition.

The problem of vandalism in old and vacant buildings is a common one and certainly a very sad commentary on the times. Actually, there are several types of vandals. Some of them are thieves known as "pickers" who illegally enter old and vacant buildings and remove anything and everything that appears to have salvage value. Among them are the "connoisseurs" who select only the choicest tid-bits such as marble and tile, fireplace mantels and so on. Often they are clumsy and inept, breaking more than they manage to salvage. Finally, there are the true vandals who simply destroy for the sake of destroying. Not content with wanton breaking, spray painting everything in sight and at last setting fire to the place is the usual finale. Offenders are rarely apprehended and when they are generally receive light sentences, if any.

A happier fate than that of the Old Shoemaker's house may be cited in the case of the Steinke house which for many years had been a point of attraction on Grand Avenue in Port Washington. Built around 1860, the attractiveness of this tiny house also was attributable to the brickbuilding idiom and the small, intimate scale. Similarly endangered by vandalism, the house nevertheless escaped serious damage and was donated to the Ozaukee County Pioneer Village by its current owners, the Werking family. It was transported bodily to the outdoor museum, was restored, and now houses replicated professional offices and a dress shop.

In the same manner and of the same period, but considerably larger and built of brick of a more reddish cast, are the Dickmann and Fick houses near Campbellsport. The Old Parsonage on the Kuehl place near Lebanon is another excellent example of this type of brickwork, with the color again running into the russet-vermilion range produced by the clay of the Hustisford area. Another outstanding example in this idiom, but carried out in buff brick, is the Demmon house near West Bend, built in 1860. Similar in color, although with some differences in treatment, is the house at 521 Main Street in Jefferson — an excellent specimen also and worthy of preservation.

DEMMON HOUSE near West Bend, east elevation.

"OLD PARSONAGE" near Lebanon, southwest elevation.

DICKMANN house near Campbellsport, southwest elevation.

FICK house near Campbellsport, southwest elevation.

ST. MICHAEL Evangelical Lutheran church near Woodland, southwest elevation.

St. Michael's Lutheran Church near Woodland and the Heart Prairie Lutheran Church on the west shore of Whitewater Lake are perhaps the two finest surviving specimens of church work employing this technique of brickbuilding. St. Michael's Church, in addition to the denticulated brick cornice, displays molded brick voussoirs in the arch rings over the openings. While St. Michael's was built by German settlers from Brandenburg in Prussia and the Heart Prairie Church by Norwegian people, the similarity in the brickwork is remarkable. Both churches were built in the 1860s, are unspoiled, and therefore excellent prospects for preservation. St. Michael's has always been known as the Machus Church — *die Machuskirche* — following an old custom of dubbing a church with the name of one of its more prominent pastors — in this case, the Reverend F. F. Machus, who served the parish from 1871 to 1900. The congregation was organized on St. Michael's Day, September 1859, and the present church building was begun in 1863 under the direction of the Reverend Philipp Wetzel. According to the old German church records, the cost of the building came to $2,200.00 — *und keine Schulden gemacht!* Two bells were bought and placed in the steeple, but not until 1897 when the congregation had saved up enough money to pay cash for them. The larger bell bears the name *Germania*, weighs 1,361 pounds and cost $286.78. The smaller bell, *Columbia*, weighs 782 pounds and cost $167.17. Originally, the windows of St. Michael's were wood muntined sash, replaced with art glass, so-called, about the turn of the century.

Most early churches were located on carefully chosen sites, but few were given as beautiful a setting as the Heart Prairie Church. Situated close to the water's edge, it is visible for miles across Whitewater Lake. Early

HEART PRAIRIE LUTHERAN CHURCH, Whitewater Lake, viewed from northwest.

parishioners living along the shores came to church in small boats, such transportation being faster and more convenient than travel by horse and wagon over muddy, rutted roads. The interior of the Heart Prairie Church is typically Norwegian with a central pulpit surrounded by a semi-circular chancel and altar rail. The little church yard adjoining the building also extends right down to the lake and contains some interesting old stones.

Early commercial and industrial buildings were also built of brick. One of the more interesting examples is the Barton Roller Mill on the Milwaukee River at Barton, now part of West Bend. Built on the site of an early saw mill, the oldest part of the present structure dates back to the mid-1860s, with Milwaukee common brick as the principal material. For many years the mill was operated by the Gadow family, producing rye and various wheat flours with its buhr stones.

The Laper Feed Mill at Fairwater is a salt box structure of very fine local red brick. It is one of the rare Wisconsin brick structures that has a molded brick watertable course at the base of the wall atop the stone foundation.

The Gothic Revival style which manifested itself best in church buildings, also left Wisconsin with a few outstanding edifices in which brick was used as the principal medium. The oldest church building in continuous use in Wisconsin is believed to be Trinity Episcopal Church at Mineral Point. The site was donated by Moses Strong, pioneer lawyer and legislator in the area, who was also a vestryman of the church. Begun in 1839 and substantially completed by 1845, this small and very interesting structure was built of the same mellow blend of local red brick as some of the houses, and accented with label moldings and belt courses of local buff limestone. Original stained glass windows with diamond panes may still be seen in this structure, which in the

BARTON ROLLER MILL at Barton on the Milwaukee River, southwest elevation.

LAPER FEED MILL at Fairwater, southwest elevation.

TRINITY EPISCOPAL CHURCH, Mineral Point, view from southeast.

ST. LUKE Episcopal church at Racine, southeast elevation.

FIRST PRESBYTERIAN church at Racine, northeast elevation.

altogether is a very well maintained church.

Perhaps the most imposing example of brick church architecture in the Greek Revival style is the First Presbyterian Church in Racine. The tower, cornice and columns are of wood, but the walls, pilasters and some of the ornamental features are of buff colored brick. This church was built in 1851 and was designed by the architect, Lucas Bradley. The feeling of the building is English, the spire being reminiscent of the London towers by Wren and Gibbs. A much more modest, but still very handsome brick church in Greek Revival style is the Presbyterian church at West Granville, now Milwaukee. Recessed arches

PRESBYTERIAN church at West Granville, northeast elevation.

and brick pilasters on the front elevation are carried out in an exceptionally careful manner. On a stone plate over the main entrance the date 1861 appears as does the inscription attesting the congregation's bilingual constituency: *Die Erste Presbyterian Kirche*.

At Racine, St. Luke's Episcopal Church is an impressive pile in the more ornate and spacious type of Gothic Revival church. Built shortly after the Civil War, it replaced an earlier structure on the same site which had been destroyed by fire. The brick is buff in color and is probably of Milwaukee origin as was the architect, Edward Townsend Mix, who had a predilection for this material. One of the unusual features is the broach-spired tower which is set on an angle. Buff limestone was used for accents which become more prominent as the brickwork continues to weather and develop a fine patina which age alone can impart.

The Gothic Revival style continued to be popular throughout the nineteenth century, and here in Wisconsin a rather austere variation of the style was developed, mostly in rural churches. The work was generally that of country masons whose knowledge of architecture may have been limited, but whose skill in the use of brick was unerring. One of these "Prairie Gothic" churches is Ebenezer Moravian Church, just south of Watertown, built in 1890. It is the third church edifice of this congregation, the first one having been a log structure and the second a "long yellow brick building," built in 1856. Church records spell out that the plan was to build the church of stone, but proper material was not to be found in the community. So, brick was used which had been brought from Milwaukee by wagon drawn by oxen. This church was built during the pastorate of its founder and first minister, the Reverend Johann Gottlob Kaltenbrunn, who was a product of the Moravian Diaspora in Silesia, Prussia, and had been a missionary to New York City before coming to Watertown in 1853. The difficulties of the early years in Wisconsin, as experienced by this congregation, were typical of the times, but by the time the present church was built, a measure of stability and prosperity had been achieved. At the time of this building, the Reverend Theobald Kant was the pastor, and the record indicates that the new church was also built of "yellow brick."

EBENEZER Moravian church, near Watertown, viewed from southeast.

ST. PAUL Evangelical and Reformed Church, at Silver Creek, southeast elevation.

SHILOH MORAVIAN CHURCH near Sturgeon Bay, view from northwest.

Not strictly classifiable as Gothic Revival, but simply somewhat Nordic in feeling and reminiscent of German and Scandinavian churches of the time, are St. Paul's Church in Silver Creek, Sheboygan County; Shiloh Moravian Church, south of Sturgeon Bay, and Mount Olive Norwegian Evangelical Lutheran Church in the same vicinity in Door County. St. Paul's is built of a tan and buff blend brick of exceptionally good color, bearing a strong resemblance to some of the early brick coming from Fond du Lac county. Atop the steeple of this very quaint structure is a wrought iron weathervane with two crossed keys, symbolizing the Office of the Keys through which forgiveness is attainable. Shiloh Church is built of the regionally popular red brick which came from Forestville in Door County. Window openings have segmental arches, and the open belfry holds a single bell. Woodwork has been painted white, as have the corner

MT. OLIVE LUTHERAN CHURCH near Sturgeon Bay, view from northwest.

bricks, to simulate quoins, and the foundation. This church was built in 1896 by a congregation composed of German and Norwegian families. Mount Olive church, a few miles to the south, is of the same *genre* as to type, materials and design; having been built in 1902. Both are eloquent witnesses to the qualities of good brickwork in otherwise modest and unassuming buildings.

The preservation of historically and architecturally significant brick buildings is generally an on-site proposition. Because of massive load-bearing walls, these buildings are extremely difficult to transport unless completely dismantled. For this reason, and except for rare exceptions, most of the smaller early brick buildings disappeared as they outlived their usefulness. Fortunately, a number of larger old buildings have remained functional, particularly as churches and residences, thus being reasonably assured of preservation. In other instances, the preservation has been a deliberate undertaking by individuals and groups. Two exceptionally important preservations of this kind are the Tallman house in Janesville and Villa Louis at Prairie du Chien. Both houses are in the flamboyant Italian villa mode, which was one of the more ornate variations of nineteenth century Victorian architecture. The Tallman house, a three story buff brick structure, was built in 1857 by William Tallman, and over the years has accumulated its share of legends, such as, Abraham Lincoln slept here and that, during the difficult days preceding the Civil War, an "underground railway" station was established here to assist escaped slaves on their way to freedom.

Villa Louis, also restored as a museum of the High Victorian period, was erected in 1872 by Hercules Dousman, one of Wisconsin's earliest tycoons. For years an argument was being made by *afficionados* of the mansion

TALLMAN house at Janesville, northwest elevation.

"VILLA LOUIS" at Prairie du Chien, southeast elevation.

RICHARDS OCTAGONAL HOUSE, Watertown. Old photograph showing view from southwest prior to restoration. Photo courtesy of Miss Gladys Mollart.

RICHARDS OCTAGONAL HOUSE, Watertown, viewed from southwest.

that the work performed in 1872 was simply a major rebuilding of an earlier house which Dousman was known to have built in 1843. As evidence of this some red brick was pointed out in the masonry walls which otherwise seemed to be uniformly buff in color. The earlier house had been built of red brick, but the size, proportions and general configuration of the two houses could never be reconciled. Finally, in going over Dousman's papers, the curator of Villa Louis discovered that there were indeed two separate buildings, and after the old red building had been torn down, Dousman ordered the brick to be salvaged for re-use in the new building, as back-up material for the Cream City brick, brought from Milwaukee, with which the walls were to be faced. This was done at the suggestion of the architect, Edward Townsend Mix, who surprisingly enough was also the contractor. Not that this was such an unusual practice at the time, since many architects entered the profession from the ranks of the practical builder in one form or another. As time went on and architects could sustain themselves as professional practitioners without finding it necessary to "work both sides of the street," contracting on the side became a questionable activity. As a matter of fact, The American Institute of Architects, founded in 1857, made it a condition of membership that no architect could thereafter engage in contracting — and E. T. Mix was a pillar of the profession. However, at the present time, the architectural profession seems to have come full circle, with great pressures being exerted on the Institute to legitimize contracting, or participating development activity, as a proper role of the architect. Needless to say, the last word has not been spoken on this issue, but the handwriting is on the wall.

Architecturally, the most imposing of Wisconsin's octagonal houses built of brick is the Richards house in Watertown, now restored and preserved by the Watertown Historical Society. Built in 1854 by John Richards, who came to Watertown from Hinsdale, Massachusetts in 1837, the originally cream colored brick building is three stories high, with an excellent view of the Rock River to the east. The fifty foot diameter plan of the building closely follows "a superior plan for a good size house" in Orson Fowler's well known treatise, *The Octagon House: A Home for All*, and attributed to William Howland whom Fowler refers to as "our engraver, who has quite an architectural taste and talent." The Richards house reflects other Fowler principles, including a central heating system with a wood burning furnace. The wall around the central core of the building consists of two four-inch tiers of brick with a four-inch space between which, in turn, is divided into flues to form chimneys and warm air risers to each of the twelve major rooms. A cistern with twenty-four inch brick walls is situated in the basement, and rain water collected from the roof was piped into it. Fowler maintained that rain water was far more healthful than well water, stating that "filtered rain water is the very best drinking water in the world . . . it was correctly observed in cholera times that only hard water districts suffered from this malady . . . I consider soft water a sure preventive for most forms of bowel complaint, and filtered rain water is the best."

The Richards house has a central spiral stairway of exceptionally good design and workmanship. Originally, the house had a continuous colonnaded porch all around the house at first and second floor levels, which also was an arrangement highly recommended by Fowler. The porch was removed some years ago and has never been replaced.

ELDERKIN HOUSE, Elkhorn, west elevation.

In Milwaukee, a most distinguished octagonal brick house once stood at 1631 North Fourth. It had been built in 1855 by Linus Dewey and also followed many Orson Fowler precepts. It was smaller and more compact than the Richards house but the common lineage was unmistakable. While no ways nor means could be found to save this excellent octagonal specimen, detailed measurements were taken before it was torn down in 1957.

Another remarkable octagonal house is located in Elkhorn. This is the so-called "Round House," built in 1856 by Edward Elderkin, an attorney from New York state, who had arrived in Elkhorn in 1839 when this community consisted of only seven houses. The walls of this house are sixteen inches thick in the basement and twelve inches thick above. The brick is buff and pink in color. A one story porch of rather ornamental scroll-saw treillage surrounds the house, and also covers a dry moat surrounding the English basement. This is another Fowler concept designed to keep the cellar fresh and well ventilated. An unusually elaborate glazed cupola, sixteen feet in height, rises from the top of the house. The cupola, as well as the roof framing, displays hewn timber members secured with wood pegs.

Several other octagonal brick houses may be found throughout Wisconsin, but few of them are in original and unaltered condition. Relatively well preserved specimens are the Quinn house on Main Street in Neenah, and the Kruel house at Horicon. Two stories high, both houses were built around 1855 of local buff brick, and represent a more modest version of the Octagon mode.

Despite Orson Fowler's eloquence on behalf of octagonal buildings and associated innovations, his style of architecture did not establish a general pattern, nor did it long survive. It was, however, one of the significant movements of the mid-nineteenth century that marked the beginning of more inventive and experimental architecture by which it was sought to organize and enclose space to meet particular needs according to logic and reasonableness rather than by formula and tradition alone.

QUINN octagonal house at Neenah, southeast elevation.

KRUEL octagon house at Horicon, northeast elevation.

Brick Veneer

Early brickbuilding in Wisconsin consisted of solid masonry in which the walls were at least eight inches thick, increasing in multiples of four inches as required by the height of the wall and the load imposed upon it. Brickmaking was an unsophisticated process in the early days even in the commercial yards, to say nothing of the many do-it-yourself enterprises that undertook to furnish brick in the rural areas of the state. Soil chemistry was imperfectly understood and finding the right kind of clay, adding the right amount of sand and water, and knowing how to properly fire the material in primitive kilns was often little more than a trial and error procedure in which experience counted for more than theory. Varying greatly in color, strength, porosity and absorption, the lack of uniformity was perhaps the greatest shortcoming which resulted in a great deal of picking and culling so the most uniformly shaped brick could be reserved for the outside face of the wall. The brick closest to the fire in the kiln were usually overburned and often misshapen, and were known as "clinkers." Units on the outside of the load of brick being fired were generally underburned, resultantly soft and friable, and called "salmon brick." Both clinkers and salmon brick were used for back-up purposes for which they were generally quite adequate. Thus, in a sense, the process of facing or veneering had begun, but the walls were still fully homogeneous.

The actual making of brick was at first a completely made-by-hand operation. Wood forms were filled with clay that had been tempered and mixed with sand, then set aside to allow the contents to shrink away from the forms which had been made wet and strewn with sand to facilitate the process. Following air drying, the brick were stacked with spaces between, and a "scove" kiln, usually of bee-

MASSART HOUSE near Casco. Detail of hewn-log wall faced with brick veneer simulating all-masonry construction.

MASSART HOUSE, near Casco. Seen from southeast showing basic hewn-log structure veneered with brick.

hive configuration, was literally built around the stack. Material for the kiln was usually broken and misshapen brick, not good for anything else, mortared together with mud. Openings had been left for firing and venting the kiln but subsequently mortared shut to retain the heat. Firing usually took ten to twelve days, with dry hardwood being used. As time went on, larger and more permanent kilns were devised, and with the use of better machinery and stiff-mud processing, the concept of "face brick" emerged. Stated another way, this material, also known as "pressed brick," with its greater uniformity of size and quality, was made to be distinguished from "common" brick.

Thus, solid brick walls, generally faced with pressed brick, remained standard practice for many decades of the nineteenth century. Somewhere around the middle of the century, however, an important departure occurred and, apparently, concomitant with the development of the platform frame and the balloon frame in wooden construction. This was the use of brick as facing, or veneer, for an otherwise completely wooden structure. The brickwork was not load-bearing, but served only to simulate a masonry structure, and at considerably lower cost. All sorts of effects were achieved architecturally, and so popular did it become that by the turn of the century, it had virtually supplanted the solid brick wall for house building, except in cases where greater fire resistance was required. But, in such instances, the newly introduced concrete block, the cinder block and the load-bearing hollow tile were apt to be used for backup instead of brick. Because this technique required fewer bricks to be used, manufacturers made great efforts to perfect the material and to produce high quality brick in a variety of colors and textures. Size, too, became standardized in the present day dimensions of 2¼ x 3¾ x 8 inches.

In attempting to determine whether an old building is solid brick masonry or simply brick veneer on a wood frame, it generally becomes necessary to open the wall for inspection, although some surface clues can usually be observed. Solid brick masonry nearly always shows some headers which serve to bond the wall together. The most popular bonds in American practice were the American or common bond, English bond, and Flemish bond. The first and most widely used, the American or common bond, has a course of headers to every five or six courses of stretchers. English bond consists of alternate courses of headers and stretchers, and Flemish bond has headers and stretchers alternating horizontally and vertically, each header being centered on the stretcher above and below. In a brick veneer wall, which is only that, there is no need for headers to bond the wall together and a simple running bond, so-called, is all that is required. There are any number of cases in twentieth century work, particularly, where brick was clipped to simulate Flemish or English bond. This practice resulted not only in a better imitation of a solid brick wall, but also produced a more interesting and textured surface. Correct diagnosis of an old wall without invasive tests has, however, been made more difficult.

One of the most curious instances of brick veneer being applied to a non-masonry structure is the old Massart house near Casco in Kewaunee County. Its outward apperance is that of a well built, two story, Belgian, red brick house, trimmed with cream colored brick in the gable ends, at the corners and at the window and door openings, but in the process of dismantling part of the building it was disclosed that the structure proper was a solid hewn log building. Whether the veneer was original or added later has not been determined, although the relationship of the foundation to the superstructure suggests that it may have been original. In any event, a most curious manifestation.

Part 3 Buildings of Stone

Fieldstone Masonry

Glaciers played an important part in shaping the surfaces of most of the land now called Wisconsin. In advancing southward, the great ice sheets had rounded off the tops of old mountain ranges and hills, had filled in some valleys, gouged out other areas, started some rivers, and formed a great basin which later became the central swamp area of the state. In retreating, the glacial ice left behind huge deposits of soil and rocks as well as thousands of lakes which make up the characteristic landscape of the northern highland area and the eastern lowlands of Wisconsin.

To the early settlers coming to Wisconsin territory, the boulder deposits scattered over a large part of the countryside must have appeared formidable. After taking down the trees, and underbrush, small clearings were made, but before they could be put to the plow, the boulders, or fieldstones, had to be removed. Many of the early settlers, particularly those of German and Irish origin, were well acquainted with fieldstones since most of northern Europe was also a glaciated land. For centuries, the people living on the northern plains of Germany along the Baltic Sea, had been using *Findlinge* for the walls of their houses, barns, mills and churches. The same practice obtained in Poland, Finland and neighboring countries, and immigrants brought their fieldstone techniques with them when they came to the new world. For the early Wisconsin settlers, many days of hard work with teams of oxen were often required to drag the boulders from just a very small area. Sometimes enormously large boulders were encountered which simply could not be removed with the available tools and equipment. Such stones had to remain in place, to be removed by a future generation with the use of dynamite blasting. All other stones were dragged to stockpiles for eventual utilization in fieldstone masonry walls or for fieldstone fences which were laid dry and surrounded many a farmer's field.

These glacially transported boulders had come from igneous and crystalline rock areas of northern Wisconsin, Michigan and Canada, and were deposited over the surface of the land to the south. As a building material they represented a great variety of kind, color and hardness. The colors were predominantly shades of red, brown, black and gray. This stone was very durable. It had withstood transport by glacier for five hundred or more miles without being crushed into sand or gravel, or ground into clay. For this reason, sandstone and limestone fragments were seldom carried very far from their place of origin.

In the earliest fieldstone construction the boulders, or "hardheads," as some settlers called them, were generally used just as they were found without any attempt to crack or split them. In working these stones into a wall, the flattest sides were selected for the bed and the surface to be exposed. Smaller stones were used to fill the voids and interstices and laid with a liberal amount of mortar. Because it was very difficult to build solid corners with round stones, dressed quarrystone and sometimes brick quoins were employed to give stability to the wall. In a few instances, the fieldstone itself was squared into a rough quoin to achieve the same purpose. Generally speaking, the work of the settlers coming from northern Germany leaned toward relatively large boulders and a minimum amount of mortar. Other German work, and that of the Irish, often shows a preference for smaller stones with a much heavier application of mortar. The Finns, arriving later in the century and being essentially timber builders *par excellence*, were inclined to split fieldstone whenever they used it. Their technique for fracturing fieldstone was to build a roaring bonfire, roll in the rocks and let them get very hot, then poke them out and dash cold water on them. Breaking along their seams, the stones were then usable in smaller, clean-cut pieces. In every case,

FIELDSTONE FENCE, Washington County. Typical fieldstone drywall enclosure built of material gathered from adjoining field.

BOULDER DEPOSIT, Dodge County. Glacial deposit of fieldstone before removal and use for many purposes.

FIELDSTONE barn under construction, near Lebanon. Old photograph showing traditional method of erecting walls. Photo courtesy of Mr. H. F. Kuether.

GROTH FIELDSTONE SILO near Cedarburg, seen from northwest.

ELA fieldstone silos near Rochester, north elevation.

however, and with or without splitting, light mortaring or heavy mortaring, the skill and judgement of the stonemason were the final determinants as to bond and textural effect to be achieved.

The period of greatest popularity for the general use of fieldstone in Wisconsin seems to have been between 1850 and 1880, although it remained in favor to some extent until the end of the century. Eventually, it became limited to barn foundations and silos. Old photographs indicate that no formwork was used in the erection of fieldstone walls, but various sized stones were carefully selected to assure the most solid bond with a minimum of voids between the stones. Examinations of old walls now in ruins or in the process of being demolished disclose the extemely tight bond that was achieved, and to which these walls owed their stability and resistance to water, wind and weather.

Among the older fieldstone silos still standing are the Ela twin silos near Rochester.

They are outstanding in every respect — aesthetically, structurally and functionally. They were built by George Ela around 1880, following the pattern of the first silos in the United States, reputedly built around 1875 in Michigan by Manly Miles who had been experimenting with vertical green fodder storage as developed in France. Each of the Ela silos is twenty feet in diameter, extending fifteen feet above ground and fifteen feet into the ground. The walls are massive fieldstone masonry, thirty inches thick. Most of the old fieldstone silos were built with a slight curvature, or entasis, in the wall to strengthen the areas where internal pressures were the greatest. Washington, Ozaukee, Dodge and Waukesha counties contain some of the finest surviving fieldstone silos in the state.

While the earliest barns in Wisconsin were usually timber structures of one kind or another, some of the settlers built large and imposing stone barns as their prosperity increased. Two almost identical barns of this type and standing across the county line road from each other, are the Ruhland barns, near Fillmore. The one to the west, on the Washington County side, was built in 1876, and the one to the east, on the Ozaukee County side, now owned by Wayne Luft, in 1879. Both barns were built into the side of a hill to allow easy access to the stock barn at the lower level as well as the hay barn above. The stonework is exceptionally well done, with fieldstone boulders obviously having been selected for size and color and laid in discernible courses even though heavily mortared. Using the tip of his trowel, the stonemason scored horizontal lines across the wall — a practice that was fairly common in fieldstone masonry of the time, and done to simulate coursed masonry or, perhaps, to deliberately provide a weak point where, if shrinkage cracks shoud occur, they would be least noticeable. The walls of the

RUHLAND-LUFT BARN near Fillmore, view from southwest.

RUHLAND-LUFT BARN near Fillmore, detail of masonry.

JUNGE BARN near Silver Creek, east elevation.

JUNGE HOUSE near Silver Creek, east elevation.

Ruhland barns are also provided with vents known as "loopholes" to assure free movement of air and prevent moisture condensation on the inside of the fieldstone walls. Quoins and voussoirs in the segmental arch-rings over the window openings are tooled Ozaukee County limestone, said to have been hauled from Cedarburg at a cost of thirty-six cents per stone, plus an equal amount for the hauling. The tooling, or bush-hammering, may have been done at the quarry, but more likely at the site by the stonemason himself, since the pattern of the tooling was often his signature — a practice going back to the guilds of the Middle Ages as a means for stonemasons to recognize each other's work. The Ruhland barns have been kept in good condition and with continued good maintenance they will remain prominent pioneer landmarks for years to come.

Similar to the Ruhland barns in many ways is the fieldstone barn on the Jerome Junge farm near Silver Creek in Sheboygan County. It was also built into the slope of a hill, but of a lesser gradient, thus requiring more of an earth ramp to reach the upper level. Treatment of the boulders as to size selection, color and coursing is very much like the Ruhland barns, but in addition to the loophole vents in the walls, the Junge barn displays some interesting lunettes which appear to be simple recesses, but may have been full openings at one time, or at least, planned to be such. At any rate, they add a great deal to the apperance of the barn. The Junge farmstead is interesting not only because of the 1876 vintage fieldstone barn, but also because of the old house, the first part of which was built by Frederick Junge in about 1856. This portion of the house, now a kitchen wing, was the original building and shows how earliest fieldstone masonry was handled. Virtually none of the stones were split and were used just as they were taken off the land. They were laid at random but well fitted, although lightly mortared. The corners were made with roughly cut pieces of fieldstone which is characteristic of the earlier work. Joined to the old fieldstone portion is a newer structure, built in 1901, which, very interestingly, is a palisaded timber house, clapboarded, and one of the better specimens uncovered in recent years. Unfortunately, both parts of the house are in a state of advanced disrepair and probably will have to be razed in the near future. The only consolation to be taken from the situation is that it does permit close inspection of the anatomy and, hopefully, the possibility of making measured drawings.

Another fieldstone barn worthy of note, although of a distinctly different order, is the old Mammer barn, located between Belgium and Port Washington in Ozaukee County. This structure, built in 1872 by Isaac Mammer, has architectonic qualities reminiscent of the traditional stone barns of France and Belgium. The fieldstone masonry is heavily pargetted with mortar, almost completely covering the stones which are of relatively small size. The corners were built of limestone ashlar and the large arched opening to the barn is trimmed with dressed limestone. It is on the arch ring that the initiails I. M. and the date appear. Unfortunately, a wing was taken off the south end of the west elevation, somewhat to the building's aesthetic detriment. In the gable end of this wing the builder had playfully placed a fieldstone with skull-like features resembling a gargoyle.

Barns built entirely of stone were never plentiful and seemed to be a manifestation of the latter decades of the nineteenth century. Using fieldstone walls for bank barns with timber superstructures remained fairly common until the World War I when this practice, too, was discontinued, with concrete block and poured concrete becoming the most favored substitutes.

MAMMER BARN near Port Washington, west elevation.

ERTELMEYER BARN, Menomonee Falls. Detail of fieldstone foundation wall, now in ruins, showing how materials were combined and bonded.

ANNALA-JANOSKA BARN and *MILKHOUSE* near Hurley, seen from west.

ANNALA-JANOSKA BARN near Hurley, detail of masonry.

There is, however, at least one important exception to all of this in terms of time, type and place. This is the all-fieldstone barn located on the Janoska place about five miles south of Hurley in the Town of Oma, Iron County. Not only is it one of the finest specimens of split fieldstone work in the state, but it is an all-stone round barn at that, making it one of the very few barns of this type in the entire country. 1917, the date of building, is also comparatively late for this type of masonry but it will be remembered that the far reaches of Wisconsin's north country were still relatively primitive areas during the early years of the present century, and building practices still obtained that had been discontinued in the southerly, more intensively urbanized areas some years before. At any rate, the all-round barn is a gem to be treasured. Local people still call it the Annala barn, because it was Matt Annala who built it. He and his wife, Hilma, had come from Finland and had been farming in Oma Township for some years when, apparently feeling themselves sufficiently prosperous to do so, they undertook to build a barn which, then as now, must have been a showplace. Matt Annala was a carpenter and a mason, as well as a farmer. That he was a skilled mechanic is evidenced by the workmanship on the barn and other buildings. The walls of the barn are solid fieldstone, two feet in thickness. The diameter of the building is sixty feet, and in the center there is a silo which has a fieldstone wall thirty inches thick on the first level and above that salt-glazed tile up to the cupola. When operative, the barn accommodated twenty-four cows, a bull and six calves. Also round in plan and built of similarly disposed solid, split-fieldstone walls is a milkhouse which was erected shortly after the barn. There is also a split fieldstone veneer farmhouse on the place, but not of pioneer vintage, having been built in 1941. Nevertheless, the whole farm group presents a harmonious appearance.

Fieldstone houses of the mid-nineteenth century often reflect Greek Revival influences in terms of floor plans and details such as doors, windows and cornices which were generally carried out in wood. But the distinctive qualities are often less those of architectural "style" then the admirable handling of the material. Sometimes fieldstone and quarried rocks were combined for very interesting effects. The old Clark house near Cedarburg is one of the finest examples of this combination. Built in 1848 by Jonathan Morrell Clark of New Jersey, the stone plate in the north gable attests both the date and the builder's name. Would that every builder had been so thoughtful. From 1870 to 1939 it was the home of the Doyle family. Catherine Doyle, a widow, was the family matriarch and one of the oldest settlers in Ozaukee County. Many stories were told about the Doyle "boys" who were reputed to have been either highwaymen, stagecoach robbers or train robbers. Whether fact or fiction, these stories persisted, and when the last of the Doyles passed away, the legend was further enhanced when a large sum of money, cached between the floor joist under some loose floor boards, had been discovered. For many years the house was known as the Doyle house rather than Clark house, and certainly not without cause. Standing on the corner of the Bonniwell Road and what was then the Cedarburg Plank Road, there was also a toll-gate at this point, the operation of which also give rise to reports of various irregularities somehow identified with the Doyle "boys." Subsequent to the Doyle family, the house was owned and occupied by other families, and also renovated and altered to some extent. The house is built of fieldstone boulders with tooled gray limestone quoins and lintels. The south front is composed of gray limestone

JONATHAN CLARK HOUSE near Cedarburg, east elevation.

SMALL BARN ON ERTELMEYER PLACE, Lisbon Road, Menomonee Falls. Note combined use of quarried limestone and fieldstone.

blocks. The limestone very probably came from one of the quarries in nearby Cedarburg and after years of weathering has taken on the characteristic blue-gray tone of the material which is light cream color when freshly quarried.

Another interesting variation of fieldstone combined with quarried rock is the old Holz house nearby, believed to have been built around 1850 by one of the O'Briens — a very prominent family in the area during the mid-nineteenth century. In this house, for reasons unclear, fieldstone was laid up to approximately the window heads of the first floor, and the wall continued with quarried rock up to the roof.

Important also is another survival of fieldstone work is the old Kopp house in Cedarburg, which was originally the home of the Lynch family. Evidently the work of Irish stonemasons of the 1850 decade, this little house — although somewhat altered and added to — possesses a very unusual charm. A short distance away, near Thiensville, the Peuschel house, also reputedly built by one of the O'Briens during mid-century, is another noteworthy specimen of fieldstone farmhouse. The Wilde house, also near Thiensville and built in 1869, shows the more florid effect gained by splitting the fieldstone and reducing the mortar joints to a minimum. One of the most colorful of the split fieldstone houses in southeastern Wisconsin is the Ziegelbauer house at St. Lawrence in Washington County, in which the stone was set with heavily mortared joints. Door and window openings were arched with handmade yellow brick. The quoins for this house were fashioned of fieldstone and are exceptionally large. According to the date stone in the south gable, the Ziegelbauer house was built in 1867. Original-

HOLZ HOUSE near Cedarburg, viewed from west.

KOPP house near Cedarburg, southeast elevation.

PEUSCHEL house near Thiensville, south elevation.

WILDE house near Freistadt, southwest elevation.

ZIEGELBAUER HOUSE, St. Lawrence, viewed from southwest.

SEEFELD *house near Mayville, southwest elevation.*

SEEFELD *house near Mayville. Detail of arched window treatment and elaborately textured fieldstone masonry.*

ly, it was a blacksmith and wagonmaker's shop with attached dwelling. Later, and for many years, the building was used as a carpenter and cabinetmaker's shop.

A flamboyancy rarely encountered in early fieldstone work may be seen in a house near Mayville, believed to have been built around 1860. For many years it was occupied by the Seefeld family and is now owned by Marvin Schellpfeffer. The walls of this house are faced with selected, highly colorful fieldstones with fairly heavy mortar pargetting and the mortar, in turn, studded with small particles of black basalt or granite which give the wall a very lively and almost playful apperance. The German counterpart of this technique was known as *Buntbau*.

Fieldstone construction was also used to good advantage in some of the earlier churches in Wisconsin. Using comparatively small boulders suffused with a heavy application of buff colored mortar, Immaculate Conception Roman Catholic church at Burlington is one of the more imposing examples. Designed by the architect, Victor Schulte, the cornerstone shows the date as 1860. While identifiable as Gothic Revival in style, this church possesses an individuality not usually associated with this period. Another church showing somewhat similar treatment of heavily mortared fieldstone masonry is St. Augustine, near Newburg in Washington County. This church was built in 1857, following the establishment of a Roman Catholic mission by Father Caspar

IMMACULATE CONCEPTION ROMAN CATHOLIC CHURCH, Burlington, viewed from southwest.

ST. PETER ROMAN CATHOLIC CHURCH near Newburg, east elevation.

Rehrl, who has been called the "Apostle of Washington County." An unusual architectural feature of this church is the octangular roof superimposed on the square wooden steeple. Located in the same vicinity is St. Peter's church, also of fieldstone, in which the mortar pargetting was scored horizontally with the tip of the trowel, presumably to simulate regular coursing. This church was built in 1861, according to the cornerstone, and is now used only as a cemetery chapel. It is one of the few known fieldstone churches with a half-octagon apse. Original wood muntined windows are still in place, as are interior fittings such as pews, altar and pulpit. On the whole, it is a distinguished landmark with much dignity and repose.

ST. AUGUSTINE ROMAN CATHOLIC CHURCH near Newburg, viewed from southeast.

ST. PATRICK Roman Catholic church near Adell, southwest elevation.

ST. PATRICK Roman Catholic church near Adell. Detail of highly colorful and textured wall of split fieldstone masonry with brick treatment at window openings.

A highly colorful and beautifully textured wall of split fieldstone masonry is that of St. Patrick's Roman Catholic church near Adell in Sheboygan County. This building was erected in 1877, and the Reverend Denis Tierney was pastor at the time. The masonry in this church is of exceptionally fine quality with a wide range of color. Accents of black are provided by split basalt boulders which are brown on the weathered surfaces. Red conglomerates and pink granite boulders are blended with dolomite blocks, some of which show interesting small fossils. Gray granite quoins and pink rock-face granite on the south front which may have been hewn from large boulders, combine for a very colorful effect with the yellow brick of the bell-cote and arch voussoirs at door and window openings. The Irish stonemasons did themselves proud on this piece of work, and it is very clear that they gave their house of worship the best they had.

Not quite as colorful and somewhat understated, but equally interesting as an example of outstanding fieldstone architecture, is St. John's Lutheran church in New Fane, Fond du Lac County, built in 1871 while the Reverend G. S. Schilling was pastor. As was frequently the case in country congregations, the members hauled the boulders to the site and assisted the master mason in the building of the walls. A unique feature of this church is that the stone sizes were graduated, becoming

ST. JOHN Evangelical Lutheran church at New Fane. East wall shows fieldstone masonry, cut limestone corner buttresses and brick treatment of cornice and window openings.

Cobblestone Work

An interesting variant of fieldstone masonry was the cobblestone wall. Medium size, egg-shaped stones, probably of glacial origin and worn round by marine or fluvial action, were carefully selected for uniformity of size and sometimes of color, and laid in even courses, apparently for visual effect rather than any other advantage. The practice of building cobblestone walls in America seems to have originated in central and northern New York state with the greatest concentration to be found within a sixty mile radius of Rochester. It is understandable, therefore, that many Wisconsin cobblestone houses were built by New York people who settled around Beloit, Burlington, East Troy and other sections of Rock, Racine and Walworth Counties. The European ancestor of the cobblestone wall very probably was the sixteenth and seventeenth century English flintwork of Suffolk and Cambridgeshire, where colorful flint and chalk fragments were alternately coursed, often with very curious effects. In the surviving Wisconsin cobblestone examples, the mass of the wall was usually fieldstone rubble, although there are a few instances in which the wall proper was built of brick. In any event, the cobblestone was applied as an outside veneer, requiring a technique that was painstaking as well as time consuming.

smaller and smaller as the courses reached the top of the wall and up into the gable. The building has a yellow brick cornice, with the same material being used as treatment around the door and window openings. Corner buttresses of dressed gray limestone were used in lieu of quoins.

Southeastern Wisconsin is the area of greatest concentration of fieldstone survivals in the state, but their number is rapidly being decimated as buildings are abandoned and left to the elements. The craftsmanship and innate aesthetic feeling for fieldstone masonry as evidenced by pioneer structures in Wisconsin may have been equalled elsewhere, but it was never excelled anywhere in the country.

A typical and extremely good example of cobblestone work is the Richardson house at Clinton in Rock County. Erected in 1843, this house very closely resembles New York prototypes. Of similar plan and disposition is the Maier cobblestone house near East Troy. Its builder was Major Spoor, an early settler who came from New York state. The house was built in 1849. A few similarly designed and built houses may still be found between Troy and East Troy, and one of the best of these is the

MAIER *cobblestone house near East Troy, southeast elevation.*

RICHARDSON *cobblestone house at Clinton, northwest elevation.*

LOOMIS HOUSE *near East Troy, east elevation.*

Loomis house, built in 1851. The Healy house in the same vicinity is a brick building built in 1850, but the cobblestone wing, unusually well designed, appears to be an earlier piece of work. The cobblestone surfacing of this wing is laid in a heavy shell of lime mortar six inches thick, over an eight inch vermilion brick backup wall. This house is believed to have been built by another member of the Spoor family, also of New York state.

In the vicinity of Rochester stands the Kempken house which was built in 1847 by Matthew Blackburn. This house was an evenly coursed cobblestone front with dressed limestone quoins, the remainder of the house walls being limestone ashlar. The cornice and trim are made of wood, as are doors and windows. The style is Greek Revival with early Victorian overtones. A somewhat purer example of Greek Revival in the Hazelo house near Rochester which was built in 1858. Despite the comparatively late date it is virtually free of Victorian aspects in addition to having some of the most unique cobblestone work in the state. On its front this house has a wall composed of egg-shaped stones which were obviously selected for size and color, and each one set into a recess made of mortar in the manner of setting a gem stone. The other walls are also laid up in limestone ashlar masonry.

HEALY house between Troy and East Troy, southeast elevation of cobblestone wing.

KEMPKEN house near Rochester, southeast elevation.

HAZELO HOUSE near Rochester. Detail of cobblestone wall with quoins.

HAZELO HOUSE near Rochester, viewed from southeast.

COBBLESTONE INN at East Troy, west elevation.

ENTERPRISE building at Palmyra, west elevation showing cobblestone wall with cut limestone store-front treatment.

In East Troy stands the Cobblestone Inn, originally known as the Buena Vista House. Also designed in Greek Revival style, this three story cobblestone tavern and hotel building was erected in 1843 by Samuel R. Bradley of Milwaukee. It is said that with his one-horse wagon he collected all the stones used in its construction from nearby river beds. The Buena Vista House was one of the leading hostelries in the area and, as such, was a favorite stopping place for political figures of the day, including Abraham Lincoln, when they traveled through this section of the state.

At Palmyra, there is a small store building with a good cobblestone front, trimmed with dressed limestone. Known at one time as the Enterprise Building, it was built in 1845 and also reflects Greek Revival stylism. A very good example of banded cobblestone is the old Dodge house at Port Washington, now serving as a gate house for the power plant of the Wisconsin Electric Power Company. The style, again, is Greek Revival, and the year of building as it appears on the date stone was 1848. The striped treatment, probably the best in Wisconsin, was achieved by laying alternate rows of stone of constrasting color — in this instance pink, black and white. The egg-shaped stones are also unusually uniform in size, suggesting that a great deal of labor must have been involved in picking them out.

The cobblestone mode, as elsewhere, was of short duration in Wisconsin, and did not in any sense constitute an architectural movement, but as a technique in the use of stone it has more than passing interest.

DODGE HOUSE, Port Washington. Detail of cornice, datestone and cobblestone masonry of exceptional quality.

The Gravel Wall

When Orson S. Fowler first addressed the question of house building reform, he did so in terms of geometrical configuration primarily, and with no particularly innovative approach to the use of building materials. All of this changed after the publication of his first treatise in 1848, in which he extolled the virtues of the octagon as the ideal planning module but, evidently, still thinking in terms of conventional construction. In 1850, in the course of a lecture tour to Wisconsin, Fowler met Joseph Goodrich, trader, innkeeper and amateur builder, who had found in the boulder studded glacial till an abundance of coarse sand, gravel and lime, from which he had made a mixture called a grout or gravel wall. Describing the discovery, Fowler wrote:

"In 1850, near Jaynesville, Wisconsin, I saw houses built wholly of lime, mixed with that coarse gravel and sand found in banks on the western prairies, underlying all prairie soil. I visited Milton, to examine a house put up by Mr. Goodrich, the original discoverer of this mode of building, and found his walls as hard as stone itself, and harder than brick walls ... Part way up, a severe storm washed it, so that a portion fell. His neighbors wrote on it with chalk by night, 'Goodrich's Folly.' But after it was up, he wrote in answer, 'Goodrich's Wisdom.' It stood; it hardened with age. He erected a blacksmith's shop, and finally a block of stores and dwellings; and his plan was copied extensively. And he deserves to be immortalized, for the superiority of his plan must certainly revolutionize building, and especially enable poor men to build their own homes. All the credit I claim is that of appreciating its superiority, applying it on a larger scale, and greatly improving the mode of putting up this kind of a wall."

In 1853, the first revised edition of Fowler's treatise was published and carried, appropriately enough, the expanded title: *A Home for All or The Gravel Wall and Octagon Mode of Building New, Cheap, Convenient, Superior and Adapted to Rich and Poor*. In his book, Fowler detailed at great length how appropriate materials for a gravel wall were to be found, how they were to be mixed, how placed to form a durable wall, and what the cost might be. Fowler's concepts of the octagon in domestic architecture and the use of natural materials caught the imagination of America, even though briefly. Fowler was a many-faceted man, a reformer and, above all, an idealist whose overriding concern was to improve the condition of Man. How well he succeeded may still be debatable but, if nothing more, he did, literally and figuratively, admit a breath of fresh air to the architectural thinking of his time.

MILTON HOUSE, Milton, viewed from west.

WOODRUFF HOUSE, Ripon, east elevation.

OCTAGON HOUSE, Fond du Lac, viewed from northeast.

The buildings with the gravel walls built in Milton, which Fowler so admired — or at least portions thereof — are still to be seen. The principal building in the group, the Milton House, is not an octagonal exemplar but a hexagonal essay. It is a three-story structure, built as a stagecoach inn, now converted to a museum and open to the public. At one time Wisconsin had a substantial number of gravel wall buildings, mostly octagonal, and among the best preserved is the Octagon House at 276 Linden Street in Fond du Lac. This fairly small house was built in 1856 and embodies many Fowler precepts in addition to the gravel wall construction. The outside of the walls was covered with rough-cast stucco applied to wood lath and wood furring strips. Whether this treatment was original has not been determined, but it seems likely that after the grout walls began to show signs of eroding the stuccoing may have been undertaken. Because of the extra thickness thus added to the wall, door and window openings had to be modified, suggesting that outside doors and window sash were replaced at that time. The front porch is also clearly an addition. Apparently, a major renovation was undertaken early in the present century. Massive limestone ashlar basement walls are original and vestiges of the Fowler-advocated cistern for rain water and the central heating system are still in evidence.

The Jacob Woodruff house in Ripon is the only remaining octagonal building in that city, and is the only known octagon house in Wisconsin built of "grout block," an early type of concrete block construction. The house is two stories high with a fairly flat pitched roof, on top of which is a widow's walk with a wooden balustrade. The house was built around 1855 by Jacob Woodruff who had come to Wisconsin from Litchfield, Connecticut in 1845, as part of the Ceresco Phalanx, a utopian Socialist Fourierite settlement established adjacent to the land which became Ripon a few years later. The Ceresco Phalanx was disbanded in 1850, but many of its members, including Jacob Woodruff, remained and became early citizens of Ripon. The Woodruff house stands on the site of the original Ceresco community. Jacob Woodruff was a blacksmith and interested in spiritism as well as horticultural experiments which may have led to his appreciation of Orson Fowler. Despite his early Socialist affiliations, he was one of the founding fathers of the Republican party — albeit an abolitionist — when it was formed in 1854.

LIMESTONE formation in Waukesha County, showing natural stratification which offered the pattern for much of the early ashlar masonry in this region.

Quarried Rock Structures

Much of Wisconsin is immediately underlain with deep limestone deposits which extend in a broad belt to the eastern, southern and western parts of the state. Varying widely in texture and composition, the stone is coarse and granular in some places, while in others it is dense and finely crystalline. Wisconsin's limestone is actually a form of dolomite because of the magnesium content in addition to calcium carbonate. However, commercial terminology supported by the geological classification of the material as Niagara limestone deposits, suggest the name to be appropriate for all practical purposes.

Large quantities of limestone were used by early Wisconsin builders, both for the lime it yielded and for the stone itself. Because of excessive porosity, softness, and the presence of deleterious minerals, not all limestone was suitable for building purposes even when taken from the same formation that may have yielded some good stone. Wisconsin limestone ranges in color from buff, cream and pink tones through various shades of warm gray to dark, bluish gray. The sandstones, often variegated, tended to range from white and ivory to tan and brown.

Early settlers made good use of both local limestone and sandstone, and in the hands of Cornish and Welsh masons, particularly fine handling was the rule. Throughout southern Wisconsin there are excellent surviving examples, although their number also decreases with each succeeding year.

Natural stratification occurs in many limestone formations. Finding the stone in layers not only facilitated removal, but also suggested the pattern for much of the early ashlar masonry. Other limestone formations, however, did not possess such laminations which meant that blocks of stone had to be broken out of solid formations, although some bed seams could usually be found to facilitate the splitting process.

MUCKERHEIDE house near Kewaskum, detail of south gable showing treatment of fenestration and stonework.

MUCKERHEIDE house near Kewaskum, southwest elevation.

An outstanding specimen of limestone masonry, in which large irregular blocks were used, is the Muckerheide house near Kewaskum. Built around 1880, the color effect is particularly good, being a combination of gray stone with a distinctly buff colored mortar heavily trowelled over the joints. In addition, surface scoring was added to simulate regular coursing. A house of similar limestone masonry construction is the old Johann Kressin place near Kirchhayn in Washington County. Interesting as a survival is the wooden lintel over the main entrance of this house which bears the German language inscription that it was built by Johann Kressin in 1855, and that the master mason was D. Ernst, and H. Gres (Graese) the master carpenter. The lintel also bears the Bible verse, Joshua 24:15, *Ich und mein Haus wollen dem Herrn dienen* — "But as for me and my house, we will serve the Lord." This inscription, or *Haus Spruch*, followed an ancient German practice. Over the door of another stone house near Newburg, a similar verse, now badly eroded, can still be deciphered as *Unsern Ein und Ausgang segne Gott* — "God bless our coming in and our going out."

JOHANN KRESSIN house near Kirchhayn, detail showing lintel at main entrance with inscribed "Hausspruch."

CEDARBURG MILL, Cedarburg, viewed from southwest.

CONCORDIA MILL, Hamilton, seen from southeast.

A distinctly local variety of limestone building developed in Cedarburg and environs during the mid-nineteenth century. Again, without too much reference to any particular "style," the type and quality of limestone masonry places this work in a class by itself. The stone was taken from local quarries and was generally of a light cream color which, upon weathering, turned to a pleasant blue-gray. Since the stone lacked pronounced laminations, it was generally cut and laid in rather large and fairly regular blocks. Laid in buff colored sand-lime mortar, a beautifully harmonious effect was achieved. Wherever dressed or cut stone was used the same native formations were utilized. Numerous houses as well as the Cedarburg Mill and the Concordia Mill in nearby Hamilton were built in this fashion. These two mills are among the few that have survived. At one time, virtually every community of consequence in southern Wisconsin possessed one of these mills, attesting the now little remembered fact that Wisconsin, before it became the nation's leading dairy state, had been one of the most important wheat producing areas in the country. The Cedarburg Mill is a five story building situated

KEHL WINERY, near Sauk City, west elevation.

KEHL WINERY, near Sauk City. Detail of main entrance and stone masonry.

on Cedar Creek. It was built by 1855 by Frederick Hilgen and William Schroeder at a cost of $2,200.00. The land had been acquired for one dollar per acre. At its peak capacity, this mill produced 120 barrels of fine white flour daily. The Concordia Mill was built in 1853 by Edward H. Janssen and after being unused for many years, was converted to a distillery during World War II.

In the hills overlooking the Wisconsin River near Sauk City stand the remains of the Kehl Winery which was built in 1867 by Peter Kehl, an immigrant German vintner. The building is constructed of yellow dolomitic limestone taken from the adjoining hills where this material can still be seen overlaying the sandstone bedrock. The Kehl Winery is a distinctly German building. In addition to its exceptionally handsome stonework, the coffered soffit and jambs of the main entrance are an unusual feature. White wine was produced here and kept in three stone-vaulted cellars in the lower level of the building. The vineyards were located on the slopes to the north of the winery. In 1899 all the vines were killed by frost and the winery operation was terminated. Long vacant, the building has been rehabilitated in recent years and, happily, a new winery has been established under new auspices.

Some of Wisconsin's finest old churches were built of locally quarried limestone and sandstone. Outstanding examples, to name but a few, are the Congregational Church at Shopiere, David Star Lutheran Church at Kirchhayn, and St. Martin Roman Catholic Church at St. Martin in Dane County. The Shopiere church was completed in 1853, with Gothic Revival style windows added in 1871. Basically a Greek Revival design, the flush wood board tower and octagonal wood belfry are reminiscent of the New England origins of the church's builders. The walls are constructed of rather large blocks of yellow limestone which abounds in the area. Appropriately enough, the name Shopiere is an Anglicized version of the French *chaux pierre*, meaning limestone. The church had a number of distinguished Rock County pioneer members, among them Louis P. Harvey, governor of Wisconsin during the Civil War.

CONGREGATIONAL church at Shopiere, northwest elevation.

David Star Church is one of the oldest Lutheran church edifices in the state, having been built in 1856 as the second building of the congregation which was founded in 1843 by immigrants from Pomerania and Silesia, both provinces of the old Kingdom of Prussia. These immigrants were of the Old Lutheran persuasion — *Altlutheraner* — who had left their homeland primarily for reasons of religious freedom. For their church they chose large blocks of gray and buff limestone — incorrectly identified in the old records as being sandstone — and laid them in rough ashlar fashion, bedded in comparatively small mortar joints with surfaces scored to imitate regular coursing. The interior has sustained two major renovations and on the outside a not altogether compatible vestibule has been added as well as an incongruous, but necessary, steel fire-escape.

The lines of St. Martin Church are quite severe and follow the rather austere variation

DAVID STAR Evangelical Lutheran church at Kirchhayn, southeast elevation.

ST. MARTIN Roman Catholic church at St. Martin, northwest elevation.

ST. MARTIN Roman Catholic church at St. Martin, detail of main portal.

of Gothic Revival which appeared in Wisconsin during the mid-nineteenth century but, again, it is the excellence of the stonework that makes the church outstanding. Here also a rather dark gray limestone was set in a distinctly buff colored mortar which blends exceptionally well and which now, together with the stone, has acquired a very pleasing patina in terms of both color and texture. St. Martin Church was built by 1861 by German immigrants from the vicinity of Trier, and occasionally a few expressions in *Triersch* can be heard, even today.

Two additional churches, but of a somewhat different order in terms of stonework, also deserve mention. They are the Sacred Hearts of Jesus and Mary Church at St. Martin's in Franklin, Milwaukee County, and St. Dominic's at Marcy in Waukesha County. Both are Roman Catholic, but Sacred Hearts was built by German immigrants and St. Dominic's by Irish. The records of Sacred Hearts congregation indicate that the construction of the church was begun in May, 1858, under the aegis of its pastor, the Reverend Franz Weinhart. The church was finished and dedicated on the 15th of October, 1859, the consecrator being the Most Reverend John Martin Henni, bishop of Milwaukee. The church was solemnly blessed under the title of *Heiligen Herzen Jesu und Maria*. Architecturally, the building strongly recalled South German and Austrian Baroque prototypes, as it was originally designed and built. The walls were laid up of large irregular blocks of local limestone, heavily pargeted with white mortar. The windows were narrow and round arched somewhat typically, but the outstanding feature was the very Baroque "onion" tower which dominated the front elevation. Such a *Zwiebelturm* was a popular hallmark of rural German and Austrian churches, but in America it was a rarity. Unfortunately, along about 1880, the congregation felt impelled to enlarge the church by extending the front, removing the old tower, and building a new Neo-

SACRED HEARTS OF JESUS AND MARY CHURCH, St. Martins, Franklin. Seen from southeast at about time of Civil War. Photo courtesy of Sacred Hearts Church.

ST. DOMINIC ROMAN CATHOLIC CHURCH, Marcy, viewed from southeast.

SACRED HEARTS OF JESUS AND MARY ROMAN CATHOLIC CHURCH, St. Martins, Franklin, viewed from southeast.

Romanesque tower with a conventional pointed steeple. The new tower was also built of local stone, cut in small and fairly regular pieces, and bedded in buff colored mortar which matches the stone.

St. Dominic's Church at Marcy was built in 1868 by a congregation that was almost solidly Irish. It is a Lannon stone structure — not alone in the generic sense the term is being applied today to most any limestone facing — but in the sense that the material actually came from the quarry at Lannon. Light gray in color, the body of church's walls are laid random ashlar with the tower stones being more mechanically disposed. The top of the tower, housing the bells, was built of wood and clapboarded. St. Dominic's Church still stands, although no services have been held in it since 1959. The interior has been altered from time to time. Whatever its future use may be, the building deserves to be saved as does the cemetery in which lie buried many of the area's pioneer Irish settlers.

CHAPEL OF ST. MARY THE VIRGIN on grounds of Nashotah House, northwest elevation.

In a class by itself, and adhering much more closely to early English prototypes than most of its Gothic Revival contemporaries, is the Chapel of St. Mary the Virgin on the grounds of Nashotah House, the Episcopal theological seminary on Nashotah Lake in Waukesha County. With its steep roof, lancet windows and stone bell-cote, the building demonstrates that simplicity can be impressive. The walls are Waukesha County limestone, laid random ashlar which must be rated among the best in an area where fine stonework is almost a commonplace. The interior of the chapel has a great deal of atmosphere and a very churchly appearance. Arranged more or less like a monastic church, the *prie-dieux* on either side of the aisle face each other to accommodate antiphonal, liturgical worship. The viability of Gothic stylism for traditional Christian services is clearly shown in this building. Construction was begun in 1859, interrupted by the Civil War, and completed around 1868. For many years the famous Gothic Revivalist, Richard Upjohn of New York City, was credited with the design of this building, but on the basis of recently uncovered information this attribution is incorrect. Upjohn did in fact supply plans and specifications, but the seminary's trustees decided to return the documents to Upjohn because the chapel would be too expensive if built according to the design submitted. Thereupon, the Milwaukee architect, James Douglas, was retained to design the chapel. James Douglas and his brother, Alexander, had one of the first architectural offices in Milwaukee and apparently had started out as carpenters. How much Upjohn's design may have influenced Douglas is not known, but for his architectural services, Douglas received $25.00.

Built by English immigrants whose taste for really good stonework was also unerring is St. Alban's Episcopal Church in Sussex. The

CHAPEL OF ST. MARY THE VIRGIN on grounds of Nashotah House, detail of west front.

congregation was founded in 1842 and the present building was started in 1864 and completed some years later. Also built of local limestone ashlar in light gray and buff tones, the church is definitely reflective of the small rural English parish church of the sixteenth century.

The use of limestone ashlar, laid random, as seen in these old churches and numerous other structures in Waukesha County was suggested by the natural rock formations themselves. This type of early stonework became the prototype for much of the subsequent so-called "Lannon" stone masonry in Wisconsin and elsewhere. The Milwaukee architect, Richard Philipp, was the first to employ this kind of stonework on some of his fine residences around the turn of the century. It was at this time that stone veneering came into popular use, as had brick veneer some years earlier, eventually displacing the massive masonry wall entirely.

In Sauk and Dane Counties, an unusual technique was developed in the treatment of both sandstone and limestone. Alternate squares of large and small stones were used to gain a very unusual and interesting effect. Probably of French origin, or at least inspiration, this method of laying stone was perfected by German stonemasons such as Caspar Steuber, in and around Prairie du Sac. A prime example of this kind of stonework developed in this locality is the Ballweg house. Near Leland in Sauk County, the small church of St. Mary of Loreto exhibits an interesting variation of the alternating squares technique. In this case the stone, golden yellow in color, was laid in a free ashlar amounting almost to rubble and overlaid with regularly spaced, raised-mortar joints, purely for effect and to imitate squared blocks of stone. The quoins and stones around the openings were, however, cut from solid blocks of limestone. Wood muntined

ST. ALBAN *Episcopal church at Sussex, west elevation.*

BALLWEG HOUSE *near Sauk City, detail showing stone pattern of alternating squares of large and small stones.*

ST. MARY OF LORETO Roman Catholic church near Leland, detail showing fenestration and unique stonework.

sash including a small rose window at the west front are of great interest. Original pews, pulpit, altar and the small semicircular altar rail may still be seen, although the church is no longer in active use. Crystal glass chandeliers and nickelplated base burners complete the interior as it must have appeared in 1880 when the church was built. Few buildings have ever been given a more beautiful setting than this little church viewed against the dark green hills of Sauk County.

ST. MARY OF LORETO ROMAN CATHOLIC CHURCH, near Leland, viewed from southwest.

Unquestionably some of the most perfect stonework to be found anywhere in the United States is that of southwestern Wisconsin. Again, sandstone and limestone were used interchangeably, with colors inclined to buff and yellow. The Doyle house near Shullsburg is a classic example of local stonework, with architectural lines identifiable as Greek Revival. The house was built around 1845 by Colonel E. C. Townsend, who had come to Wisconsin from Kentucky. He raised horses and had a race-track on the premises. The house is built of grayish-buff limestone ashlar and the south front consists of large blocks of light gray "glass rock," found deep in the lead mines of the area.

At Platteville, the Mitchell-Rountree house has been a landmark since 1837 when it was built by the Reverend Samuel Mitchell who came to Wisconsin from Virginia some years earlier. The walls of this house are buff dolomitic limestone in fairly large blocks, covered with buff stucco. The stone was fitted very closely and in some places mud joints were used instead of mortar. Of Tidewater Virginia Colonial design, the house contains five fireplaces and some well-detailed mantelpieces and other fine interior trim. The floors are random width ash boards. Miss Laura Rountree who lived to be ninety-five years of age was a lineal descendant of the Reverend Mitchell. She was born in the house and spent her entire life in it. During her last years, she conveyed the house to the Grant County Historical Society but retained the right of life tenancy. Following her death the society refurbished the house and made some necessary repairs, and now operates it as a museum which is open to the public.

At Mineral Point some of Wisconsin's finest stonework may still be observed, although by no means in the quantity of even thirty years ago. Mineral Point could still

DOYLE *house near Shullsburg, west elevation.*

MITCHELL-ROUNTREE *house at Platteville, south elevation.*

TRELAWNEY and PENDARVIS houses at Mineral Point, northeast elevation facing Shakerag Street.

INGRAHAM HOUSE, Mineral Point, viewed from northeast.

become Wisconsin's Williamsburg, if indifference and eventual neglect do not preclude the possibility. Some outstanding restoration efforts must be noted, however, particularly in the work Robert Neal and Edgar Hellum did on the Trelawny and Pendarvis houses in Shakerag Alley. These buildings were recently taken over by the State Historical Society of Wisconsin and have become museums. These houses had been built by Cornish miners about 1830. The fronts are cut limestone blocks laid with very thin joints and the backs are random ashlar. A typical one-story miner's cottage is the Ingraham house which was similarly faced with dressed stone on the front and ashlar on the sides and back. The Bracken house, also in Mineral Point and the same time frame, has the same kind of stone treatment, but is otherwise Greek Revival and a good example of that style. Also, it appears that the builder was a German stonemason, rather than a Cornishman. Thus it could be surmised that the nature of the material itself suggested the most appropriate treatment, transcending tradition and ethnic preference. Another Greek Revival house of some importance in Mineral Point is the Moses Strong house, which is an unusual architectural composition particularly in the treatment of its interesting gables. This house was built in two stages — the first part around 1845 and the second about 1860 — both by Moses Strong, one of Wisconsin's early political figures as a lawyer and legislator. Along High Street in Mineral Point, a number of excellent stone-faced store buildings have survived. Some of them have been allowed to deteriorate but none of them are beyond repair. Being as unique as they are, their restoration and preservation should rate the highest priority.

Unusual stonework, recalling that of eastern England, is the alternate coursing of wide and narrow bands of squared limestone block such as found in the vicinity of Fond du

BRACKEN HOUSE, Mineral Point, view from southwest.

MOSES STRONG house at Mineral Point, southwest elevation facing Fountain Street.

OLD STONE FRONTS of commercial buildings on High Street, Mineral Point.

HAMILTON house near Fond du Lac, detail of wall showing alternating courses of limestone ashlar and cut stone label molding at lintel.

HAMILTON house near Fond du Lac, east elevation of main gable.

Lac. Local limestone of excellent quality and color handled in this manner is the Hamilton house just south of Fond du Lac. Tooled limestone lintels, window sills and label moldings add to the charm and character of this stonework.

Limestone ashlar was also used for barns and other farm buildings, although not nearly as frequently as fieldstone. One of the largest and most imposing of these is the old Wyman barn at Shopiere. Originally, the lower level of this building was used as a sheep barn. It was built in 1857 by an early settler named McGrath, and measures forty feet by one-hundred feet in size. Equally large and imposing but of somewhat later date is the Thomas barn near Barneveld in Iowa County. It was built in 1881 by three immigrant Welsh stonemasons who quarried the gray limestone blocks and laid up the walls. Near Mt. Horeb in Dane County the Syvstestad barn, built in 1860 by a Norwegian immigrant, is another example of massive limestone construction in agricultural architecture.

WYMAN barn near Shopiere, northeast elevation.

THOMAS BARN, near Barneveld, southeast elevation.

SYVSTESTAD STONE BARN, near Mount Horeb, seen from northwest.

BAUER *lime kiln at Knowles, southwest elevation.*

BAUER *lime kiln at Knowles, detail of limestone masonry.*

TRIMBORN *lime kiln at Greendale, southeast elevation.*

During the nineteenth century almost every community in the limestone areas of the state had a lime kiln in connection with the quarry. In the days before Portland cement, all mortar and plaster mixtures were predominently lime, although some of the lime was obtained from clam shells taken from streams. Of the few lime kilns still standing even though no longer in use, perhaps the most impressive, architecturally, is the old Bauer lime kiln near Knowles in Dodge County. Picturesque as buildings, the craftsmanship of the stonework is superb. The Trimborn lime kiln likewise displays a fine appreciation of masonry craftsmanship. Located near Greendale in Milwaukee County, this kiln is the last of five kilns built around 1850. It, too is in ruinous condition but steps have been taken recently to begin a process of restoration and preservation.

In addition to buildings of all sorts, Wisconsin stone was used effectively in other structures, especially bridges. Few of these remain, having been replaced by steel and concrete structures, but an excellent survival is the old nine-arch bridge over the Sheboygan River near St. Cloud. The arches are of particularly good proportion and the entire structure has a distinctly architectural feeling. The same can be said of the old arched bridge spanning the Shioc River — a tributary of the Wolf — at Shiocton. Perhaps the oldest surviving stone bridge of consequence, is the five-arch railroad bridge over Turtle Creek near Tiffany in Rock County. It was built in 1869 and the designer was a Chicago engineer named Van Mienen. Peculiarly enough no local stone was employed in this bridge, despite the fact that local limestone was available in unlimited quantities. It seems, however, that local stone while plentiful was not regarded as being sufficiently strong to support the load the bridge was to carry. Accordingly, the foundation stone was shipped in from Waupun and the superstructure stone from Duck Creek, near Green Bay. When the bridge was built, the largest locomotive in use weighed forty-three tons. Modern locomotives weigh upwards of two hundred and fifty tons. For this reason, the arch rings have been reinforced with concrete.

As is the case with brick and other masonry structures, the preservation of stone buildings having architectural or historical significance is generally a matter of on-site treatment. Fortunately, continuing functional usefulness helps to assure the preservation of some of the best of the old churches and residences, but the loss of stone mills and lesser buildings is so rapid that few will survive unless positive steps are taken to place them in protective custody, pending the time when means and opportunities become available to restore and preserve them. To retain these tangible links with Wisconsin's historic past is still in the realm of possibility, but the time for affirmative action grows alarmingly short. May the hope be once more expressed that the people of Wisconsin will act to keep their precious cultural legacy — for themselves and for posterity — before time runs out.

STONE bridge over Sheboygan River near St. Cloud, west elevation.

STONE BRIDGE over Shioc River, Shiocton, viewed from south.

STONE railroad bridge over Turtle Creek near Tiffany in Rock County.

Photo Index

Michael Ahner House / Saukville, Ozaukee County   5*
Annala-Janoska Barn & Milkhouse / Hurley, Iron County   90
Backenstoe-Howard House / Cooksville, Rock County   69
Baird Law Office / Green Bay, Brown County   46
Balfanz House / Prairie du Sac, Sauk County   49
Ballweg House / Sauk City, Sauk County   111
Barton Roller Mill / West Bend, Washington County   73
Bauer Lime Kiln / Knowles, Dodge County   118
Bavry House / Carlsville, Door County   11
Beck Haybarn / Maple, Douglas County   13
Bergen House / Norway, Racine County   8*
Blashka House / Maribel, Manitowoc County   17
Bracken House / Mineral Point, Iowa County   115
Braemer House / Hustisford, Dodge County   36
Cedarburg Mill / Cedarburg, Ozaukee County   105
Chapel of St. Mary the Virgin / Nashotah Lake, Waukesha County   110
Chiviok Barn / Phillips, Price County   12
Christian Barn / Watertown, Dodge County   38
Christianson Barn / Deerfield, Dane County   59
Jonathan Clark House / Cedarburg, Ozaukee County   92
Clausing Barn / Eagle, Waukesha County   58**
Cobblestone Inn / East Troy, Walworth County   100
Collins House / Caledonia, Racine County   44
Commercial Buildings / Mineral Point, Iowa County   115
Concordia Mill / Hamilton, Ozaukee County   105
Congregational Church / Shopiere, Rock County   107
Cooper House / Waterford, Racine County   48
Cotton House / Green Bay, Brown County   44
Cornelius Barn / Shawano, Shawano County   24
David Star Evangelical Lutheran Church / Kirchhayn, Washington County   107
Davidson Windmill / Lakeside, Douglas County   13

Demmon House / West Bend, Washington County   71
Dickmann House / Campbellsport, Fond du Lac County   71
Dodge House / Pt. Washington, Ozaukee County   100
Dorn House / Baileys Harbor, Door County   27
Dousman-Dunkel-Behling House / Brookfield, Waukesha County   50
Doyle House / Shullsburg, Lafayette County   113
Duncan House / Cooksville, Rock County   68
Eaton House / Mineral Point, Iowa County   65
Ebenezer Moravian Church / Watertown, Jefferson County   75
Ela House / Rochester, Racine County   48
Ela Fieldstone silos / Rochester, Racine County   86
Elderkin House / Elkhorn, Walworth County   80
Ertelmeyer Barn / Menomonee Falls, Waukesha County   89, 92
Enterprise Building / Palmyra, Jefferson County   100
Fick House / Campbellsport, Fond du Lac County   71
First Baptist Church / Merton, Waukesha County   52
First Presbyterian Church / Racine, Racine County   74
Freitag Barn / Monticello, Green County   57
Goodrich Cabin / Milton, Rock County   7
Grignon House / Kaukauna, Outagamie County   49
Groth Fieldstone Silo / Cedarburg, Ozaukee County
Hakala Barn / Maple, Douglas County   21
Hamilton House / Fond du Lac, Fond du Lac County   116
Hashek Barn / Myra, Ozaukee County   9***
Hauge Church / Daleyville, Dane County   14
Hawks Inn / Delafield, Waukesha County   50
Hazelo House / Rochester, Racine County   99
Healy House / East Troy, Walworth County   99
Heart Prairie Lutheran Church / Whitewater Lake, Walworth County   72

Hermann-Braun Barn / Baileys Harbor, Door County   29
Hilgendorf House / Freistadt, Ozaukee County   37
Holy Innocents Church / Nashotah, Waukesha County   56*
Holz House / Cedarburg, Ozaukee County   93
Hoxie House / Cooksville, Rock County   69
Immaculate Conception Roman Catholic Church / Burlington, Racine County   95
Ingram House / Mineral Point, Iowa County   114
Ison Stovewood Barn / Crandon, Forest County   25
Johann Kressin House / Kirchhayn, Washington County   104
Junge Barn / Silver Creek, Sheboygan County   88
Junge House / Silver Creek, Sheboygan County   88
Kehl Winery / Sauk City, Sauk County   106
Kempken House / Rochester, Racine County   99
Ketola House / Oulu, Bayfield County   8**
Klessig House / Fillmore, Washington County   39
Kopp House / Cedarburg, Ozaukee County   93
Koivu Barn / Maple, Douglas County   12
Krause House / Kirchhayn, Washington County   33
Johann Kressin House / Kirchhayn, Washington County   104
Krueger House / Kirchhayn, Washington County   35
Kruel House / Horicon, Dodge County   81
Kuehneman House / Racine, Racine County   44
Kuenzi Barn / Watertown, Dodge County   38
Lammi Barn / Maple, Douglas County   12
Langholff House / Watertown, Dodge County   32
Laper Feed Mill / Fairwater, Fond du Lac County   73
LaPlant Barn / Lena, Oconto County   26
Lehmann House / Richfield, Washington County   70*
Loomis House / East Troy, Walworth County   98
Lueder-Laack Barn / Plymouth, Sheboygan County   60
Lueskow-Mueller House / Iron Ridge, Dodge County   38**
Maier House / East Troy, Walworth County   98
Mammer Barn / Pt. Washington, Ozaukee County   89
Massart House / Casco, Kewaunee County   82

Mastey Barn / Angelica, Shawano County   24
Mecikalski Boarding House & Saloon / Lennox, Oneida County   22
Meidenbauer House / New Berlin, Waukesha County   10
Meinhardt Bank / Burlington, Racine County   67
Methodist Church / Green Lake, Green Lake County   53
Milton House / Milton, Rock County   101
Moravian Church / Green Bay, Brown County   53
Muckerheide House / Kewaskum, Washington County   104
Muskego Meetinghouse / Prospect, Waukesha County   52
Mitchell-Rountree House / Platteville, Grant County   113
Mt. Olive Lutheran Church / Sturgeon Bay, Door County   76
Norwegian Barn / Stoughton, Dane County   57*
Octagon House / Fond du Lac, Fond du Lac County   102
Octagonal Barn / Hollandale, Iowa County   58
Jonas Ojala House / Oulu, Bayfield County   11
Old Parsonage / Lebanon, Dodge County   71
Painesville Chapel / Franklin, Milwaukee County   51
Parlow House / Waubeka, Ozaukee County   67
Pearson Barn / Maple, Douglas County   19
Penttila Barn / Maple, Douglas County   20
Petty Cabin / Aztalan, Jefferson County   6
Peuschel House / Thiensville, Ozaukee County   93
Plank-Schuler House / Brillion, Calumet County   16, 17*
Polster House / Mayville, Dodge County   66
Issac Porter House / Cooksville, Rock County   69
Presbyterian Church / Milwaukee, Milwaukee County   74
Quinn House / Neenah, Winnebago County   81
Rezek Palisaded Barn / Maribel, Manitowoc County   18
Richards Octagonal House / Watertown, Dodge County   78
Richardson House / Clinton, Rock County   98

Roi-Porlier-Tank House / Green Bay, Brown County 30
Ruhland-Luft Barn / Fillmore, Washington/Ozaukee Counties 87
Ruokonen Barn / Maple, Douglas County 21
Rupnow Barn / New Glarus, Green County 57
Sacred Hearts of Jesus & Mary Roman Catholic Church / Franklin, Milwaukee County 109
St. Alban Episcopal Church / Sussex, Waukesha County 111
St. Augustine Roman Catholic Church / Newburg, Washington County 95
St. Augustine Roman Catholic Church / New Diggings, Lafayette County 42, 55
St. Dominic Roman Catholic Church / Marcy, Waukesha County 109
St. John Chrysostom Episcopal Church / Delafield, Waukesha County
St. John Evangelical Lutheran Church / New Fane, Fond du Lac County 97
St. Luke Episcopal Church / Racine, Racine County 74
St. Martin Roman Catholic Church / Franklin, Milwaukee County 108
St. Mary of Loreto Roman Catholic Church / Leland, Sauk County 112
St. Michael's Lutheran Church / Woodland, Dodge County 72
St. Patrick Roman Catholic Church / Adell, Sheboygan County 96
St. Paul's Evangelical Lutheran Church / Woodland, Dodge County 41*
St. Paul Evangelical & Reformed Church / Silver Creek, Sheboygan County 76
St. Peter Roman Catholic Church / Milwaukee, Milwaukee County 54**
St. Peter Roman Catholic Church / Newburg, Washington County 95
St. Wenceslaus Church / Waterloo, Jefferson County 15
Sanford-Duerst / Whitewater, Walworth County 47
Sauna, abandoned / Maple, Douglas County 13
Schreiber Barn / New Berlin, Waukesha County 60
Schulz-Zirbel House / Iron Ridge, Dodge County 34**

Scotch Covenanter Meetinghouse / Vernon, County
Scotch Meetinghouse / Dover, Racine County 51
Seefeld House / Mayville, Dodge County 94
Seventh Day Baptist Church / Albion, Dane County 52
Shiloh Moravian Church / Sturgeon Bay, Door County 76
Steinke House / Pt. Washington, Ozaukee County 70***
Stone Bridge / Shiocton, Outagamie County 119
Stone Bridge / St. Cloud, Fond du Lac County 119
Stone Railroad Bridge / Tiffany, Rock County 119
Moses Strong House / Mineral Point, Iowa County 115
Syvstestad Barn / Mt. Horeb, Dane County 117
Tallman House / Janesville, Rock County 77
Thomas Barn / Barneveld, Iowa County 117
Trelawney & Pendarvis House / Mineral Point, Iowa County 114
Trimborn Kiln / Greendale, Milwaukee County 118
Trinity Episcopal Church / Mineral Point, Iowa County 73
Trinity Evangelical Lutheran Church / Freistadt, Ozaukee County 41*
Turck-Schottler House / Kirchhayn, Washington County 6**
Vauk House / Freistadt, Ozaukee County 10
Villa Louis / Prairie du Chien, Crawford County 77
Vomastic House / Waukechon, Shawano County 18
Wade House / Greenbush, Sheboygan County 49
Wade House / Mineral Point, Iowa County 65
Weissenfluh House / Ridgeway, Iowa County 11
Whitaker-Lurvey House / Dousman, Waukesha County 68
White Pillars / De Pere, Brown County 47
Whitney Barn / Pittsville, Wood County 60
Wilcox Barn / Angelica, Shawano County 24
Wilde House / Freistadt, Washington County 93
Woodruff House / Ripon, Fond du Lac County 102
Wyman Barn / Shopiere, Rock County 117
York House / Zenda, Walworth County 46

Zachow House / Baileys Harbor, Door County   28
Zettler House / Waubeka, Ozaukee County   37***
Ziegelbauer House / St. Lawrence, Washington
   County   93

  *Building now demolished.
 **Building now in Old World Wisconsin, near Eagle.
***Building now in Ozaukee County Pioneer Village,
   near Waubeka.